HEIDEGGER:
THE CRITIQUE OF LOGIC

HEIDEGGER:
THE CRITIQUE OF LOGIC

by

THOMAS A. FAY

MARTINUS NIJHOFF / THE HAGUE / 1977

ISBN 90 247 1931 3

PRINTED IN BELGIUM

TABLE OF CONTENTS

PREFACE

Since his inaugural lecture at Freiburg in 1929 in which Heidegger delivered his most celebrated salvo against logic, he has frequently been portrayed as an anti-logician, a classic example of the obscurity resultant upon a rejection of the discipline of logic, a champion of the irrational, and a variety of similar things. Because many of Heidegger's statements on logic are polemical in tone, there has been no little misunderstanding of his position in regard to logic, and a great deal of distortion of it. All too frequently the position which is attacked as Heidegger's is a barely recognizable caricature of it.

Heidegger has, from the very beginning of his career, written and said much on logic. Strangely enough, in view of all that he has said, his critique of logic has not been singled out as the subject of any of the longer, more detailed studies on the various aspects of his thought. There is, therefore, a need for a detailed presentation of precisely what Heidegger understands by logic, what role he accords to it, how it figures in his overall thought, what logic he "attacks" (if he does so), and why, in terms of the larger perspectives of his overall thought, he should hold the position that he does. Our first purpose in this work will therefore be to attempt to determine what Heidegger understands by logic, and in this way, it is to be hoped, to help to clear away some of the confusion which presently prevails regarding it.

It may seem to some that the logic-question is not terribly important to his overall thought, but if it is recalled that for Heidegger the foundation of logic is λόγος, and that λόγος constitutes one of the most fundamental aspects of Being, as well as being the foundation of language, the importance of the logic-question becomes apparent. Further, Heidegger has noted that since 1934 the logic-question has been transformed into the language problematic, and the importance of language to the thought of the late Heidegger could scarcely be overestimated. Therefore when we make notions such as λόγος, logic, and language

the object of our inquiry, we are dealing with questions which are very
close to the heart of Heidegger's thought. And, as we hope to show,
what is involved in Heidegger's critique of logic is nothing less than
a total transformation of the way of conceiving of the nature of
philosophy.

The English translations of Heidegger's texts that occur are my own;
I have given the German text in the footnotes so that the reader who
might wish to compare the translation with the German text might
easily do so. This has also permitted me to handle the translations
with a greater degree of freedom, attempting to render what seemed to
me to be the best sense of Heidegger's texts. A list of the abbreviations
of Heidegger's works, together with the facts of publication will be
found immediately preceding the text. All of the italics which occur,
unless otherwise noted, are those of the author of the text in question.

LIST OF ABBREVIATIONS

ED   *Aus der Erfahrung des Denkens.* Pfullingen: Neske, 1954.
FW   *Der Feldweg.* 3rd ed. Frankfurt am Main: Klostermann, 1962.
SG   *Der Satz vom Grund.* 2nd ed. Bern: Francke, 1954.
DF   *Die Frage nach dem Ding.* Tübingen: Niemeyer, 1962.
EM   *Einführung in die Metaphysik.* 2nd ed. Tübingen: Niemeyer, 1958.
HD   *Erläuterungen zu Hölderlins Dichtung.* 2nd ed. Frankfurt am Main: Klostermann, 1951.
G   *Gelassenheit.* Pfullingen: Neske, 1959.
HH   *Hebel—der Hausfreund.* 2nd ed. Pfullingen: Neske, 1958.
HW   *Holzwege.* 3rd ed. Frankfurt am Main: Klostermann, 1957.
ID   *Identität und Differenz.* Pfullingen: Neske, 1957.
KM   *Kant und das Problem der Metaphysik.* 2nd ed. Frankfurt am Main: Klostermann, 1951.
KTS   *Kants These über das Sein.* Frankfurt am Main: Klostermann, 1962.
KB   *Die Kategorien- und Bedeutungslehre des Duns Scotus.* Tübingen: 1916.
LU   *Die Lehre vom Urteil im Psychologismus. Ein kritisch-positiver Beitrag zur Logik.* Leipzig: 1914.
N   *Nietzsche.* 2 vols. Pfullingen: Neske, 1961.
PW   *Platons Lehre von der Wahrheit.* 2nd ed. Bern: Francke, 1954.
SZ   *Sein und Zeit.* 8th ed. Tübingen: Niemeyer, 1957.
HB   *Über den Humanismus.* Frankfurt am Main: Klostermann, 1947.
US   *Unterwegs zur Sprache.* Pfullingen: Neske, 1959.
WG   *Vom Wesen des Grundes.* 4th ed. Frankfurt am Main: Klostermann, 1955.
WW   *Vom Wesen der Wahrheit.* 3rd ed. Frankfurt am Main: Klostermann, 1954.
VA   *Vorträge und Aufsätze.* Pfullingen: Neske, 1954.
WD   *Was heisst Denken?* Tübingen: Niemeyer, 1961.
WM   *Was ist Metaphysik?* 7th ed. Frankfurt am Main: Klostermann, 1949.
WP   *Was ist das—die Philosophie?* Pfullingen: Neske, 1956.
ZS   *Zur Seinsfrage.* Frankfurt am Main: Klostermann, 1956.
NF   "Neuere Forschungen über Logik," *Literarische Rundschau für das katholische Deutschland,* XXXVIII (1912), cols. 465-472, 517-524, 567-570.
P   "Vom Wesen und Begriff der Φύσις," *Wegmarken.* Frankfurt am Main: Klostermann, 1967.

INTRODUCTION

In 1927, with the publication of *Being and Time*, Martin Heidegger burst upon the philosophic scene with a dramatic suddenness and impact that can now be scarcely imagined. Already during the early years at the University of Freiburg, where he became *Privatdozent* in 1915 and remained until he accepted the chair of philosophy at Marburg in 1923, Heidegger had attracted attention as a lecturer. In his writing, however, following the *Habilitationsschrift*, *Die Katagorien- und Bedeutungslehre des Duns Scotus*[1] in 1915, there is a period of quiescence of some 12 years before the appearance of *Sein und Zeit* in the *Jahrbuch für Philosophie und phänomenologische Forschung*[2] in 1927, which left the philosophic world quite unprepared for the thought that was then germinating. In the year 1928 Heidegger was offered the chair of philosophy at Freiburg, to succeed Husserl, with whom he had been closely associated from 1916, when Husserl accepted the chair at Freiburg, till Heidegger's departure for Marburg in 1923. And now, at the height of his fame, Heidegger returned as a conquering hero to the scene of his old student days for his inaugural lecture as professor of philosophy, before the assembled faculties of this great university. Gathered before him in *Plenarsitzung* were the most eminent men of the natural and social sciences,[3] all eagerly awaiting the message of the widely acclaimed author of *Sein und Zeit*. And what was the theme of Heidegger's now famous inaugural lecture directed to this audience of distinguished scientists? Nothing![4] He will speak to them about "nothing" — of which

---

[1] *Die Kategorien- und Bedeutungslehre des Duns Scotus*, (Tübingen: Mohr, 1916). Hereafter, KB.

[2] Martin Heidegger, "Sein und Zeit", *Jahrbuch für Philosophie und phänomenologische Forschung*, VIII (1927), 1-438. Hereafter, SZ.

[3] *Zur Seinsfrage* (Frankfurt a. M.: Klostermann, 1956), p. 37. Hereafter, ZS.

[4] *Was ist Metaphysik*, 7th ed. (Frankfurt a. M.: Klostermann, 1949), p. 27. Hereafter, WM.

science wishes to know? nothing.[5] Science has as its constant concern beings (*Seiende*),[6] but never treats of "the Nothing" (*das Nichts*).[7] The philosopher, however, must seek after Being (*Sein*),[8] which is not-a-being (*Nicht-Seiende*).[9] But since Heidegger wishes to forestall any possible confusion of Being with the beings with which science is concerned, he will speak of this Being which is not-a-being as the Nothing (*das Nichts*).[10] But one might reasonably object, is it not a manifest piece of nonsense and a blatant violation of all of the rules of logic to attempt to treat of "the Nothing", since the very attempt to treat of it must somehow presuppose that it *is*?[11] It would seem that the principle of contradiction, which is the cornerstone of logic, is at stake here, and indeed logic itself.[12]

Heidegger was not unaware of this difficulty, and in what has become perhaps his most celebrated "attack" on logic, he responded to the anticipated objection as follows.

...The Nothing is the source of negation and not the other way around. If this breaks the might of understanding in the field of questioning into the Nothing and Being, then the fate of the dominance of "logic" in philosophy is also decided. The very idea of "logic" disintegrates in the whirl of a more primordial questioning.[13]

But why was it that Heidegger should have been led to make such an obviously provocative statement concerning logic. There would seem to be two reasons. First, if one recalls the general philosophic atmosphere at the time of the inaugural address, it becomes much easier to see why

---

[5] WM, p. 27.

[6] ZS, p. 37.

[7] WM, p. 26.

[8] Throughout this work we shall translate "das Sein" as "Being", using the majuscule, "B", to distinguish it from "das Seiende", which will be rendered by "being" with the miniscule, "b". For a more detailed analysis concerning the difficulties in rendering adequately *Das Sein* and *das Seiende* see especially William Richardson, *Heidegger: Through Phenomenology to Thought* (The Hague: Martinus Nijhoff, 1963), pp. 4, 10.

[9] WM, p. 45.

[10] WM, p. 45.

[11] WM, p. 27. Cf. also *Nietzsche*, 2 vols. (Pfullingen: Neske, 1961), II, p. 51. Hereafter, N. Also *Einführung in die Metaphysik*, 2nd ed. (Tübingen: Niemeyer, 1958), pp. 18-19. Hereafter, EM.

[12] WM, p. 28.

[13] "...das Nichts ist der Ursprung der Verneinung, nicht umgekehrt. Wenn so die Macht des Verstandes im Felde der Fragen nach dem Nichts und dem Sein gebrochen wird, dann entscheidet sich damit auch das Schicksal der Herrschaft der 'Logik' innerhalb der Philosophie. Die Idee der 'Logik' selbst löst sich auf im Wirbel eines ursprünglicheren Fragens." (WM, pp. 36-37.)

Heidegger should have been led to say the rather uncomplimentary things about logic which he did. Wittgenstein, it will be remembered, had published the *Tractatus* in 1921, and in this extremely influential work he has asserted that metaphysics is nonsense.[14] The impact of the *Tractatus* was very considerable, especially through the Vienna Circle, and especially as it was popularized by A. J. Ayer in *Language, Truth and Logic*. All of which is to say that the movement of logical positivism which reduced metaphysics to nonsense statements was gaining considerable momentum. Since Heidegger, at least at this time, could still regard his work as foundational ontology, it is not altogether surprising that he was not terribly well disposed toward logic. There is also a second reason. Heidegger in his major early work SZ had been concerned with raising anew the question of the sense of Being or Being as truth.[15] In his interrogation into the Being-question he had found that one being, Dasein,[16] had afforded a privileged access to Being, and within the analysis of Dasein itself the fundamental mood (*Grundstimmung*) of Angst had provided a very rich field of investigation. Further this mood of Angst was set into motion as Dasein encountered the Nothing (*das Nichts*). If, therefore, Heidegger had discovered that the phenomenological analysis of Angst and its relation to the Nothing had yielded such rich results for the Being-question, and if logic with its principle of contradition reduced the Nothing to nonsense, it becomes clear why Heidegger should say that the dominance of logic must be broken. It must yield to a more fundamental questioning. By the very fact that the rules of logic preclude even the possibility of a meaningful questioning about the Nothing, logic's fate has been decided.

The above statement from the *Antrittsvorlesung* is not merely an isolated one, the product of a momentary pique. Many statements of a similar vein are to be found throughout his writings, as we shall see.

---

[14] *Tractatus Logico-Philosophicus*, Trans. Pears and McGuinness (London: Routledge and Kegan Paul, 1961). See for example 2.172, 2.174, 4.003, 4.12, 4.121.

[15] We will make this equation between the sense of Being and Being as truth throughout. For its textual justification in Heidegger see for example his explanation of the "Sense of Being" in *Über den Humanismus* (Frankfurt a. M.: Klostermann, 1947), p. 25. Hereafter, HB.

[16] Dasein is a term of wide meaning in German. It may be translated as existence, being, life, presence, etc. Heidegger, however, uses it only to designate human-being. At times he separates the adverbial prefix "da" from the basic "Sein" to indicate that he wishes the term to be understood in the etymological sense of "there-being", or "being-there". For the most part I will not translate it, since it has by now become a *terminus technicus*, except in those places where clarity would seem to dictate translation.

We have simply selected what is probably the most famous one from many of a similar nature, for the purpose of introducing the logic problematic in Heidegger's thought. What we must first of all determine, it would seem, is precisely what Heidegger understands by logic. When he "attacks" logic, which "logic" is it that he is attacking? The word "logic" is, after all, placed in quotation marks which would seem to indicate that it has some special sense. But what is that sense? Does Heidegger wish to totally uproot reason, to give philosophy up to the capricious rule of feeling and instinct, to end, finally, in a nihilistic irrationalism, or sterile *Wortmystik*, as some critics indeed claim that he does. Hence our first purpose will be to attempt to see what Heidegger understands by logic. It is surprising indeed, given the interest and the amount of attention that Heidegger has devoted to logic,[17] that there have been no major studies devoted to this much neglected and much misunderstood area of his thought.[18] Heidegger from the very beginning of his philosophic career has interested himself in it. Indeed his first publication of 1912, *Neuere Forschungen über Logik*[19] was devoted to it. But because of the polemical nature of many of Heidegger's

---

[17] That Heidegger has manifested a considerable interest in logic from the very beginning of his philosophic activity becomes evident when one studies the catalogue of his published works and university lectures. Already in 1916, in the second semester of his career as a university professor we find a seminar offered by Heidegger at Freiburg entitled: "Übungen über Texte aus den logischen Schriften des Aristoteles." In 1922 a lecture course, "Phänomenologische Interpretation ausgewählter Abhandlungen des Aristoteles zur Ontologie und Logik"; 1925-1926 a lecture course, "Logik," and a seminar on Hegel's *Logik*; 1926-1927 a seminar, "Ausgewählte Probleme der Logik (Begriff und Begriffsbildung)"; 1927 a seminar, "die Ontologie des Aristoteles und Hegels Logik"; 1928 a lecture course, "Logik"; 1928-1929 a seminar, "die ontologischen Grundsätze und das Kategorienproblem"; 1933 a seminar, "der Satz von Widerspruch"; and in 1934 a course, unpublished, on logic. Here we have limited ourselves to those titles only in which the word logic itself occurs.

[18] This need has been noted for example by Rolf-Dieter Hermann who remarks: "The one factor, however, which has either been relatively or completely ignored in this controversy is Heidegger's peculiar relation to logic. Yet this relationship of Heidegger's to the field of logic — and this is a further, very important peculiarity — has been alive and manifest from the Duns Scotus publication of 1916 right up to the present day, to the appearance of Heidegger's large scale Nietzsche-interpretation of 1960. The phenomenon has been the subject of not one single article or book ..." ("Heidegger and Logic," *Sophia*, XXIX (1961), (353). The need for such a study is also noted by Albert Borgmann, "Heidegger and Symbolic Logic," in *Heidegger and the Quest for Truth*, ed. with Introduction by Manfred Frings (Chicago: Quadrangle, 1968), p. 159, note 1.

[19] *Literarische Rundschau für das katholische Deutschland*, XXXVIII (1912), Cols. 465-472, 517-524, 567-570.

statements, it is very easy to misinterpret them. Frequently the position which is criticized as Heidegger's is a badly distorted version of it. Therefore, one of our purposes in undertaking this work is to attempt to determine just exactly what Heidegger's position on logic is, and how his statements about it are to be interpreted. In this way, it is to be hoped, some of the rather massive misunderstanding surrounding his position will be cleared away.

Our approach will not be a genetic one, since a number of admirable works of this type already exist.[20] For the most part, then, we shall prescind from questions of development, the problem of the relation of the early to the late Heidegger and so on, except where they have an important bearing on the language-logic problematic, as they do for example in the transformation of the logic-question into the language problematic. We shall also presuppose in the reader a familiarity with Heidegger's thought, and hence we shall not attempt to deal in any detailed sort of way with the general themes of his thought, except where they have a direct bearing on the language-logic problematic. We will therefore take up in the opening chapter the question of the "forgetfulness of Being" because we shall see that this has a very definite relation to the logic-question. So also in the second chapter will we touch upon certain central themes of SZ, such as the existential constitution of Dasein, since this relates to the foundation of logic and the proposition which forms such an important area of investigation in logic. And so on with the remainder of the work. We shall treat of only those elements in Heidegger's thought which are necessary for an understanding of the language-logic question. But although this may seem to be a task of rather narrow scope, perhaps of quite limited importance in relation to the overall thought of Heidegger, I should like to suggest that this may not be the case. If one recalls that for Heidegger logic, at least in the authentic sense, is a reflection on λόγος (*Besinnung auf den* λόγος),[21] and that λόγος is both the ultimate ground of language, and indeed another name for it, the importance of the language-logic problematic to the thought of Heidegger becomes apparent. So that although we have taken as our point of departure, in order to introduce the logic-question, a text from the inaugural lecture which

[20] See for example William Richardson, *Heidegger: Through Phenomenology to Thought* (The Hague: Martinus Nijhoff, 1963); Otto Pöggeler, *Der Denkweg Martin Heideggers* (Pfullingen: Neske, 1963); Fernand Courturier, *Monde et être chez Heidegger* (Montréal: Presses de L'Université de Montréal, 1971).
[21] *Die Frage nach dem Ding* (Tübingen: Niemeyer, 1962), p. 122. Hereafter, DF.

may be of limited significance to the thought of Heidegger, still when one recalls that after 1934 the logic-question has been transformed into the language-question, and that this same language problematic is the central preoccupation of the late Heidegger, it can be readily seen that logic is not merely of peripheral interest to his thought. And further, although this study addresses itself expressly to the question of logic and its role in the thought of Heidegger what is really involved is no less than Heidegger's very notion of philosophy itself. The point at issue is not simply to determine the role of logic in his thought, and its possible compatibility, or incompatibility with logic as it is presently understood and practiced. This, of course, is our immediate concern. But since, in Heidegger's view, the whole history of Western philosophy has been a forgetfulness of Being, and since this has been caused by the deformation of truth as revelation (ἀλήθεια) into propositional truth, and by the degeneration of λόγος as first experienced by the early Greeks into logic, which since Plato has held philosophy in a conceptual straight-jacket which prevented the possibility of experiencing Being, the "overcoming" of logic will be the overthrow of one whole way of conceiving of philosophy, the way it has been conceived in the West since Plato. What is at issue here, then, is not simply the question of Heidegger's critique of logic, important as this might be. What is really at stake is a much larger question — the very nature of philosophy itself.

CHAPTER I

LOGIC AND THE FORGETFULNESS OF BEING

Heidegger, as is well known, was concerned from the very beginning of his way with the question of the sense of Being (*die Frage nach dem Sinn von Sein*). His thought was enkindled by the question, which in his view, has run as a *leitmotif* throughout the history of Western metaphysical thought, the question that was raised by Aristotle: τί τὸ ὄν, what is being?[1] His awareness of the Being-question, he tells us, was first awakened by a reading of Franz Brentano's dissertation, *On the Manifold Sense of Being in Aristotle*, while still a gymnasiast in Constance in the summer of 1907.[2] Before the question of the sense of Being, which his reading of Brentano's dissertation had occasioned, could explicitly be raised with any degree of clarity a gestation period of more than ten years would be required. As Heidegger notes in recalling the beginning of his way in his letter to Richardson:

Meanwhile a decade went by and a great deal of swerving and straying through the history of Western philosophy was needed for the above question to reach even an initial clarity.[3]

From the beginning, closely related to the Being-question, was the question of language and logic.

I know only this: because the reflection on language and Being determined the way of my thought from the beginning, therefore the discussion of it remained, for the most part, in the background. Perhaps this is the basic lack of SZ that I dared to go too far too early.[4]

---

[1] See his letter to Richardson, which appears as the Preface to Richardson's book, *Through Phenomenology* ..., p. XI. See also *Unterwegs zur Sprache* (Pfullingen: Neske, 1959), p. 92, Hereafter, US.

[2] *Was heisst Denken* (Tübingen: Niemeyer, 1961), p. 145. Hereafter, WD. *Was ist das — die Philosophie* (Pfullingen: Neske, 1956), pp. 24-25. Hereafter, WP.

[3] "Letter to Richardson," *Through Phenomenology* ..., p. X.

[4] "Ich weiss nur dies eine: Weil die Besinnung auf Sprache und Sein meinen Denkweg von früh an bestimmt, deshalb bleibt die Erörterung möglichst im Hintergrund. Vielleicht

In the early phase of his writing, for example in the *Habilitationsschrift*, the language-question emerged as the question concerning logic and the relation of logic to language.[5] The more limited question raised in the report of 1912, "What is logic?"[6] is broadened and deepened in the *Habilitationsschrift* of 1916, and Heidegger begins to ask about the originating source of language.[7] The foundational question is becoming more clearly evident.

It is encumbent upon philosophy of language to set forth the ultimate *theoretical* foundations upon which language rests.[8]

By the time of the publication of SZ in 1927 Heidegger saw his task clearly as a foundational work: the question of the sense of Being which gave the initial impetus to his thought is explicitly raised, and in Heidegger's view, raised for the first time in the history of ontology.[9] The sense of Being, or Being as truth, has been forgotten throughout the long history of Western metaphysics, from Plato and Aristotle[10] to our own day. It becomes necessary, then, to raise this question anew. In terms of the logic problematic, by way of a preliminary statement, we might note that the foundational question requires that the proposition treated in logic be investigated on the ontological level.[11] Symbolic logic also requires such a "founding," or ontological interpretation.

Binding and separating may be formalized still further to a "relating." In symbolic logic judgment gets dissolved into a system in which they are "co-ordinated" with one another; it becomes the object of a "calculation" but does not become the theme of ontological interpretation.[12]

---

ist es der Grundmangel des Buches 'Sein und Zeit', dass ich mich zu früh zu weit vorgewagt habe," (US, p. 93).

[5] That the reflection on the relation of logic and language already interested Heidegger at the time of the *Habilitationsschrift* can be seen for example in the following question which Heidegger poses in KB: "Dieses Beisammen von logischem Gehalt und sprachlicher Gestalt drängt zur Frage: inwieweit sind die letzteren in die Logik einzubeziehen?" (KB, p. 108.)

[6] NF, Col. 466.

[7] KB, p. 162. Cf. also WD, p. 100, and US, p. 93.

[8] "Ihr obliegt die Herausstellung der letzten *theoretischen* Fundamente, die der Sprache zugrunde liegen." (KB, p. 163.) Heidegger's emphasis.

[9] SZ, pp. 1-2.

[10] SZ, p. 2.

[11] SZ, pp. 154, 214.

[12] "Verbindung und Trennen lassen sich dann weiter formalisieren zu einem 'Beziehen.' Logistisch wird das Urteil in ein System von 'Zuordnungen' aufgelöst, es wird zum Gegenstand eines 'Rechnens,' aber nicht zum Thema ontologischer Interpretation." (SZ, p. 159.)

We shall leave this question of the problem of the foundation of logic undeveloped for now, since in order to understand Heidegger's position on this point, we must first elaborate the more general theme of the forgetfulness of Being (*Seinsvergessenheit*) and its relation to the foundation of metaphysics.

On the first page of SZ Heidegger states that his purpose in undertaking this monumental work is to raise anew the question of the sense of Being (*Sinn von Sein*),[13] since it is precisely this, the most fundamental ontological question,[14] which has been dead and buried since Plato and Aristotle.[15] The whole history of Western metaphysics has simply been a record of the forgetfulness of the sense of Being, or Being as Truth.[16] It is Heidegger's purpose to reawaken the quest after the sense of Being, or, put differently, to interrogate Being as truth-process. It is important to note, since the expressions will be recurring constantly, that Heidegger equates the expression "sense of Being" (*Sinn von Sein*) and "truth of Being" (*Wahrheit des Seins*). Thus he remarks in *Letter on Humanism*:

Whether the reflection on Being as the absolutely transcending already names the simple essence of the truth of Being, that and that alone is first and foremost the question for a thinking which attempts to think the truth of Being. Therefore it is said on p. 230 (SZ) that only from the "sense," i.e. from the truth of Being, can it be understood how Being is.[17]

It is Heidegger's contention, then, that the history of Western metaphysics has been a record of the forgetfulness of Being (*Seinsvergessenheit*). Here it may be well, first of all, to anticipate an obvious objection.

---

[13] "Und so gilt es denn, die Frage nach dem Sinn von Sein erneut zu stellen." (SZ, p. 1.)

[14] SZ, p. 437.

[15] Indeed the first sentence of SZ, p. 2, states that the question concerning the sense of Being is today forgotten. See also, *Was ist Metaphysik*, 7th ed. (Frankfurt a. M.: Klostermann, 1949), pp. 8-12. Hereafter, WM. *Einführung in die Metaphysik*, 2nd ed. (Tübingen: Niemeyer, 1958), p. 130. Hereafter, EM. *Über den Humanismus* (Frankfurt a. M.: Klostermann, 1947), p. 26. Hereafter, HB. *Holzwege*, 3rd ed. (Frankfurt a. M.: Klostermann, 1957), pp. 39-40. Hereafter, HW.

[16] WM, p. 11. Cf. also *Kants These über das Sein*. (Frankfurt a. M.: Klostermann, 1962), pp. 8-9. Hereafter, KTS.

[17] "Ob jedoch die Bestimmung des Seins als des schlichten Transcendens schon das einfache Wesen der Wahrheit des Seins nennt, das und das allein ist doch allererst die Frage für ein Denken, das versucht, die Wahrheit des Seins zu denken. Darum heisst es auch S. 230, dass erst aus dem 'Sinn', das heisst aus der Wahrheit des Seins, zu verstehen sei, wie Sein ist." (HB, p. 25.) Cf. also, WM, p. 18. *Vom Wesen der Wahrheit*, 3rd ed. (Frankfurt a. M.: Klostermann, 1954), p. 26. Hereafter, WW. Also William Richardson, "Heidegger and the Problem of Thought" *Revue Philosophique de Louvain*, LX (1962), 70.

If Heidegger has characterized the whole history of Western philosophy as an exercise in *Seinsvergessenheit*, it would seem that one could quite reasonably condemn such an attitude as the most insufferable sort of intellectual arrogance. Being has been forgotten, it is to be supposed, by the greatest thinkers of the West for some two thousand years or more, by Plato, Aristotle, Descartes, Kant, Hegel,[18] etc., and only now at this late date in history has it happened that Martin Heidegger alone of all of the greatest thinkers in the history of the West must recall philosophy to its true task. Such an objection would be based upon a misunderstanding of Heidegger's purpose in reflecting on the history of Western metaphysics. It would certainly be a misconception of what he is attempting in his questioning of the tradition to see it as a sort of sophomoric refutation of the errors which previous philosophers had made. And yet this misconception of his position occurs all too readily. As he remarks concerning historical questioning:

To question historically means: to set free and into motion the happening which is quiescent and bound in the question. To be sure such a procedure can easily be misunderstood. It could be understood as if it were a question of attributing the original determination of the thing to error or at least to shortcoming and incompleteness. This would be a childish game of vain and conceited superciliousness which all those who come later, simply because they come later, might presume to play in respect of those who have preceded them.[19]

In order to obviate this misunderstanding it is necessary, therefore, to sketch out at this point, if only in barest outline, Heidegger's concept of history as *Seinsgeschichte* (Being-history).

The forgetfulness of Being has not been caused by a failure of intelligence on the part of an Aristotle, a Hegel or a Kant. These men were, all of them, landmarks in the history of western thought.[20] Nor has the failure to think Being in its difference been due to an oversight

---

[18] EM, pp. 130-131. For an examination of the "forgetfulness of Being" by Thomas Aquinas see my article, "Heidegger on the History of Western Metaphysics as Forgetfulness of Being: A Thomistic Rejoinder," *Atti del Congresso internazionale Tommaso d'Aquino nel suo VII° Centenario*, vol. II, 480-484.

[19] "Geschichtlich fragen meint: das in der Frage ruhende und gefesselte Geschehen frei — und in Bewegung setzen. Allerdings unterliegt ein solches Vorgehen leicht einer Missdeutung. Man könnte meinen, es käme darauf an, der anfänglichen Unvollständigkeit nachzurechnen. Das bliebe ein kindisches Spiel der leeren und eitlen Überlegenheit, die sich alle Spätergekommenen, nur weil sie später kommen, gegenuber den Früheren jederzeit anmassen können." (DF, pp. 36-37.) Cf. also *Nietzsche* (Pfullingen: Neske, 1961), I, pp. 168-170. Hereafter, N. WD, p. 127; SZ, pp. 19-20; and also Otto Pöggeler, "Sein als Ereignis", *Zeitschrift für philosophische Forschung*, XIII (1959), 560, 600.

[20] WD, p. 148; KTS, p. 36; EM, p. 92.

of metaphysics.[21] Being has not, as it were, been misplaced by metaphysics and metaphysicians like an umbrella by an absent-minded professor. The cause of the forgetfulness of Being as truth must rather be sought first of all in the very essence of Being itself, which reveals itself but at the same time conceals itself.

The forgetfulness of Being belongs to the essence of Being which by its nature veils itself.[22]

and

Being itself withdraws itself in its truth. It conceals itself in its truth and hides itself in its concealing.[23]

Hence the forgetfulness of Being is not due to a mistake, or simple negligence on the part of metaphysics or metaphysicians,[24] but constitutes an e-vent, (Ereignis),[25] in Seinsgeschichte.

The forgetfulness of the difference with which Being-history begins in order to consummate itself in it, is, nevertheless, not a lack, but the richest and most far-reaching event in which Western world history comes to issue. It is the event of metaphysics.[26]

It is due, on the one hand, to the very greatness of the origin (Anfang) of thought itself[27] in which Being revealed itself in such an overpowering richness that the very effulgence of its revelation[28] could not be retained in its pristine power;[29] and, on the other hand, it is due to the fact that in its revelation Being conceals itself.[30] It sends (schicken) itself

[21] WD, p. 98; HW, p. 244.

[22] "Die Vergessenheit des Seins gehört in das durch sie selbst verhüllte Wesen des Seins," (HW, p. 336). Cf. also Der Satz vom Grund 2nd ed. (Bern: Francke, 1953); pp. 111-114. Hereafter, SG.

[23] "Das Sein selbst entzieht sich in seine Wahrheit. Es birgt sich in diese und verbirgt sich selbst in solchem Bergen." (HW, p. 244.)

[24] HB, p. 20; WD, p. 42.

[25] Following the translation of Ereignis suggested by Richardson, in Through Phenomenology ..., p. 614, which takes the English word 'event' in its etymological sense, from the Latin e (ex), and venio, to come forth.

[26] "Die Vergessenheit des Unterschiedes, mit der das Geschick des Seins beginnt, um in ihm sich zu vollenden, ist gleichwohl kein Mangel, sondern das reichste und weiteste Ereignis, in welchem die Abendländische Weltgeschichte zum Austrag kommt. Es ist das Ereignis der Metaphysik." (HW, p. 336.)

[27] HW, p. 63; EM, p. 119.

[28] Vorträge und Aufsätze (Pfullingen: Neske, 1954), pp. 227, 229. Hereafter, VA. See also WD, p. 167.

[29] Zur Seinsfrage (Frankfurt a. M.: Klostermann, 1956), p. 33. Hereafter, ZS. See also EM, pp. 12, 111, 145-146.

[30] HW, p. 310.

to man.[31] It is grasped in authentic thought,[32] and this thought is a happening (*Geschehen*) of Being. Thought then brings Being to expression in language[33] which becomes a record of Being's revelations, or history (*Geschichte*).[34] Being as truth, ἀλήθεια, is simultaneous revelation[35] and concealment,[36] that is, it sends itself and at the same time withdraws itself.[37]

Being-as-history is the destining of Being which sends itself to us, and at the same time withdraws its essence.[38]

Here in the play on words which is employed with the words *geschehen* (to happen), *schicken* (to send), *Geschichte* (history), and *Geschick* (destiny),[39] we see an example of the marvelous richness of Heidegger's use of language. It may be well to note, too, that in harkening back to the roots of such words as *Geschichte* in *schicken* and *geschehen*, the sage of the Black Forest is not simply exercising himself in word-games,[40] but rather that the procedure of going back to the primordial

---

[31] Here we cannot enter into a detailed examination of such very rich Heideggerian notions as *Geschichte*, *Geschick*, *schicken*, etc. For an excellent summary see William Richardson, S. J., "Heideggers Weg durch die Phänomenologie zum Seinsdenken," *Philosophisches Jahrbuch*, LXXII (1965) 385-396. This article is a summary of Richardson's larger work cited above, *Through Phenomenology* ....

[32] SG, p. 147; KTS, p. 34; N, I p. 528; N II, p. 484; VA, p. 231; ID, p. 18; HW, pp. 194, 60, 61, 303; HB, pp. 5, 42, 43, 46, 47; WP, p. 43; WM, p. 50; WD, pp. 85, 119, 120, 125, 126, 127, 139, 145, 136, 147, 172.

[33] HB, pp. 5, 16, 30; SG, p. 147; WP, pp. 32, 33, 35, 36, 40, 44, 45. *Hebel — Der Hausfreund*, 2nd ed. (Pfullingen: Neske, 1958), pp. 19, 25, 26, 29. Hereafter, HH.

[34] SG, pp. 119-120, 144, 147; HD, p. 35; VA, pp. 63-64; N, II, pp. 28, 483, 490. On the relation of *Geschick*, *geschichtlich*, and *Geschichte* to *Sein*, Helmut Kuhn remarks: "Dies ist aber nicht ein dem Denken zufällig unterlaufender Fehler sondern sein Geschick. Die Verkennung des Seins geschieht, ist geschichtlich, oder vielmehr, ist Geschichte. Dies ist nun zunächst nicht ein bloss menschliches Geschehen sondern eine Geschichte, die sich mit dem Sein selbst begibt. Es ist das Sein, welches 'ausbleibt'. "Heideggers 'Holzwege'," *Archiv für Philosophie*, IV (1952), 261.

[35] *Kant und das Problem der Metaphysik*, 2nd ed. (Frankfurt a. M.: Klostermann, 1951), p. 115. Hereafter, KM. *Gelassenheit* (Pfullingen: Neske, 1959), p. 61. Hereafter, G.

[36] WD, p. 8.

[37] VA, pp. 134-135.

[38] "Seinsgeschichte ist das Geschick des Seins, das sich uns zuschickt, indem es sein Wesen entzieht." (SG, p. 108.) See also ZS, pp. 33, 108-109, 147; SG, p. 130.

[39] In this connection see especially Richardson, *Through Phenomenology* ..., p. 435, note.

[40] Thus Karl Löwith, Heidegger's former student, charges him with playing an empty word-game after the manner of the glass pearl game in Herman Hesse's famous novel. He remarks in *Heidegger: Denker in dürftiger Zeit* (Göttingen: Vandenhoeck & Ruprecht, 1960), p. 15: "Heideggers Sprache ist, was er selbst mit Hölderlin von ihr sagt: 'das

meaning of the words is suggested by the concept of history itself[41] —
Being reveals itself to thought, is expressed in language, but because
it is concealment as well as revelation, the original power of the word
as expressing Being is quickly lost.

Is this return arbitrariness or an empty game? Neither the one nor the other.
If we speak of a playing here, then we do not play with words; rather the
essence of language plays with us and not only in this case, not only today,
but since long ago and continually. Language plays with our spoken language
in such a way that it readily allows it to slip away into the more obvious and
superficial meanings of the words. It is as if man had to make an effort to
authentically dwell in language. It is exactly as if the dwelling succumbed to
the danger of everydayness resistlessly.[42]

This brings us to a final point in our brief outline of the notion of
Seinsgeschichte, which is preliminary to our discussion of Being and
the Nothing, that is, Being's ἐποχή. Forgetfulness of Being in its
difference has characterized the Western metaphysical tradition, but this
is not to be construed as a failure on the part of metaphysics,[43] or
metaphysicians. It is rather an event or epoch, in the sense of ἐποχή,
in Being's history.

We can call this clearing-holding-back of the truth of its essence the ἐποχή
of Being. This word which is taken from the linguistic usage of the Stoa does not,
however, have the meaning here which it has in Husserl ... The epoch of Being
belongs to Being itself. It is thought from out of the experience of the forgetfulness
of Being.[44]

---

unschuldigste aller Geschäfte,' ein Glasperlenspiel mit Worten, und zugleich 'der Güter
Gefährlichstes.' Ihre Gefahr ist, dass sie verfänglich ist, und darum mehr fesselt als befreit."

[41] Walter Bröcker makes this point in "Heidegger und die Logik," *Philosophische
Rundschau*, I (1954-56), 49: "Man sieht, dass die Bedeutungsgeschichte des Wortes Sein
für Heidegger eine Verfallsgeschichte ist." See also Bertrand Rioux, *L'Être et la vérité
chez Heidegger et S. Thomas d'Aquin* (Paris: Presses Universitaires de France, 1963),
pp. 119-121.

[42] "Ist diese Rückkehr Willkür oder Spielerei? Weder das eine noch das andere.
Wenn hier schon von einem Spiel die Rede sein darf, dann spielen nicht wir mit Wörtern,
sondern das Wesen der Sprache spielt mit uns, und nicht nur im vorliegenden Fall,
nicht erst heute, sondern längst und stets. Die Sprache spielt nämlich so mit unserem
Sprechen, dass sie dieses gern in die mehr vordergründigen Bedeutungen der Worte
weggehen lässt. Es ist, als ob der Mensch Mühe hätte, die Sprache eigentlich zu bewohnen.
Es ist, als ob gerade das Wohnen der Gefahr des Gewöhnlichen am leichtesten erliege."
(WD, p. 83.) See also WD, pp. 42, 84, 89, 90, 91, 110, 122, 168; HW, pp. 302, 343;
ID, pp. 44, 45; KM, pp. 182, 183, 185; PL, p. 25; KTS, pp. 7, 32, 34; WP, pp. 15, 20,
31, 44; EM, pp. 38, 55, 111, 134; DF, pp. 22-24.

[43] HW, p. 43.

[44] "Wir können dieses lichtende Ansichhalten mit der Wahrheit seines Wesens die

It is an essential feature in the destiny of metaphysics that its own ground eludes it,[45] and this, because of the very nature of truth as ἀλήθεια, which is a sending of Being, but at the same time a withdrawal into concealment — "Being withdraws itself, as it reveals itself in a being."[46] Hence the very inception of thought begins with a forgetfulness of Being;[47] and even in the great period of the dawning of thought where Being is grasped in its openness by a Parmenides or a Heraclitus the full richness of Being is not comprehended.

Nowhere do we encounter a thinking that thinks the truth of Being itself and thus the truth itself as Being. This is true even of pre-Socratic thought, which as the origin of Western thought prepared the unfolding of metaphysics through Plato and Aristotle ... with the forgetfulness of Being.[48]

The forgetfulness of Being which has characterized metaphysics, then, is an epochal event in the history of Being which corresponds to Being's ἐποχή, or concealment.[49]

Thus, while it would be misunderstanding of Heidegger's position on the forgetfulness of Being of a fundamental sort to interpret it as a kind of indictment of Western metaphysics, still this assertion that the history of metaphysics has been the history of the forgetfulness of Being seems, at best, to be paradoxical. From its beginnings with Plato and Aristotle it seems that metaphysics has had as its singular preoccupation the question of the meaning of Being.[50] Indeed, the opening words of SZ are a quotation from Plato which concerns the meaning of a being (ὄν). What, then, is the meaning of the alleged forgetfulness of Being?

Metaphysics has, obviously, been concerned with beings in the sense of the ὄν ᾗ ὄν, a being as a being,[51] but what it has failed totally

---

ἐποχή des Seins nennen. Dieses dem Sprachgebrauch der Stoa entnommene Wort nennt hier jedoch nicht wie bei Husserl .... Die Epoche des Seins gehört ihm selbst. Sie ist aus der Erfahrung der Vergessenheit des Seins gedacht." (HW, p. 311.)

[45] WM, pp. 10-11.

[46] "Das Sein entzieht sich, indem es sich in das Seiende entbirgt." (HW, p. 311.)

[47] WD, pp. 4-5.

[48] "Nirgends begegnet uns ein Denken, das die Wahrheit des Seins selbst und damit die Wahrheit selbst als das Sein denkt. Sogar dort ist dieses nicht gedacht, wo das vorplatonische Denken als der Anfang des abendländischen Denkens die Entfaltung der Metaphysik durch Plato und Aristoteles vorbereitet ... Die Geschichte des Seins beginnt und zwar notwendig *mit der Vergessenheit des Seins.* (HW, p. 243.)

[49] VA, p. 71; HB, p. 23; HW, pp. 244-245; SG, p. 110.

[51] WM, p. 11.

[51] Heidegger remarks for example in WM, p. 19: "Die Metaphysik bewegt sich im Bereich des ὄν ᾗ ὄν. Ihr Vorstellen gilt dem Seienden als dem Seienden."

to grasp is the difference between Being and beings.[52] It is the clarification of this "ontological difference" between Being and beings which is the very heart of Heidegger's work.[53] Being, as distinguished from beings, is never itself *a* being.[54] Yet, while not itself *a* being, it is never separated from beings. It is the very process of truth, by which beings are lit up and appear — the coming-to-pass of the ontological difference.[55] It is the emerging-into-presence-and-abiding,[56] the gathered-together-gathering-letting-lie-forth-in-openness,[57] the process of disclosing which at the same time conceals.[58] We shall for the moment leave these three aspects of Being, that is, as φύσις, as λόγος, and ἀλήθεια, unthematic, since their explication will occupy us very shortly. It is sufficient for our purpose here to note that metaphysics has failed completely to grasp Being.

Accordingly, how does metaphysics comport itself to Being itself? Does metaphysics think Being itself? No, never.[59]

---

[52] VA, p. 71; N, II, p. 350; *Identität und Differenz* (Pfullingen: Neske, 1957), pp. 46-47. Hereafter, ID.

[53] As Albert Dondeyne has pointed out in "La différence ontologique chez M. Heidegger," *Revue Philosophique de Louvain*, LVI (1958), 35: "Les nombreuses publications parues depuis les Holzwege (qui sont de 1950), en particulier la dernière en date: Identität und Differenz ne font que confirmer toujours davantage que la 'différence ontologique' c'est-à-dire la différence qui à la fois unit et sépare l'étant et l'être (Seiende und Sein), représente vraiment le thème central de l'œuvre heideggérienne, celui qui lui confère son sens et, partant, l'unité de son mouvement." Cf. also A. De Waelhens, *Chemins et impasses de l'ontologie heideggérienne* (Louvain: Nauwelaerts, 1953), p. 5; M. Müller, *Existenzphilosophie im Geistigen Leben der Gegenwart* (Heidelberg; Kerle, 1964), p. 75ff; William Richardson, "Heidegger and Theology," *Theological Studies*, XXVI (1965), 91.

[54] "Das Sein ist niemals ein Seiendes." Cf. also ZS, p. 38: "Das Sein 'ist' so wenig wie das Nichts"; and also KTS, p. 35: "Sein kann nicht *sein*. Wurde es sein, bliebe es nicht mehr Sein, sondern wäre ein Seiendes."

[55] William Richardson, S. J., "Heidegger and God — and Professor Jonas", *Thought*, XL (1965), 27-28.

[56] EM, pp. 76-77. See also EM, pp. 11, 12, 47, 77, 83, 87-88, 105-106, 139; WD, pp. 143, 149; VA, pp. 141, 227; SG, pp. 111, 154; DF, pp. 53, 64.

[57] VA, pp. 215-216. See also VA, pp. 207-229; EM, pp. 94-104, 128-146; HW, pp. 162-163, 243, 301; HB, p. 34.

[58] Among the many places where Heidegger speaks of this, see for example: HW, pp. 43, 49, 310, 311; EM, pp. 47, 77, 78, 87, 88; N, II, p. 486; ID, p. 65; WD, 98. *Platons Lehre von der Wahrheit*, 2nd ed. (Bern: Francke, 1954), pp. 26, 32, 33, 41, 42, 43. Hereafter, PL.

[59] "Wie verhält sich dementsprechend die Metaphysik zum Sein selbst? Denkt die Metaphysik das Sein selbst? Nein und niemals." (N, II, pp. 345-346.)

While it has indeed interested itself with being (ὄν, ὄντα), it has failed totally to grasp Being in its unique distinction from beings.

By its own essence as metaphysics it is excluded from the experience of Being; for it always represents a being (ὄν) only in that which has already manifested itself of Being in a being as a being (ᾗ ὄν). Metaphysics, however, is never concerned with what has already concealed itself even in this ὄν, insofar as it was unconcealed.[60]

In a word, it has failed to grasp Being in its truth, nor does it recall truth as unconcealedness, nor the nature of unconcealedness. The truth with which metaphysics is concerned is a derivative type of truth, truth as couched in the proposition.

Metaphysics in its answers to its question about a being as such has always antecedently represented Being. It expresses Being necessarily and hence continually. But metaphysics does not bring Being itself to language because it does not bethink itself of Being in its truth, nor truth as unconcealment, nor the essence of unconcealment. The essence of truth always appears to metaphysics only in the derivative form of the truth of knowledge and the assertions which express it.[61]

It moves in the sphere of the ὄν ᾗ ὄν, that is, it treats of beings as beings,[62] but never considers Being itself — "Metaphysics, insofar as it constantly only represents a being as a being, does not recall Being itself."[63] It does not think Being as a truth-process by which Being reveals itself as it lights up beings, and yet in the very process of revelation conceals itself. But Being itself is not to be naively considered as something apart from beings, somewhat like a Platonic Idea, nor

---

[60] "Als Metaphysik ist sie von der Erfahrung des Seins durch ihr eigenes Wesen ausgeschlossen; denn sie stellt das Seiende (ὄν) stets nur vor, was sich als Seiendes (ᾗ ὄν) schon von diesem her gezeigt hat. Die Metaphysik achtet jedoch dessen nie, was sich in eben diesem ὄν, insofern es unverborgen wurde, auch schon verborgen hat. (WM, p. 20.)

[61] "Die Metaphysik hat in ihren Antworten auf ihre Frage nach dem Seienden als solchem vor diesem schon das Sein vorgestellt. Sie spricht Sein notwendig aus und darum ständig. Aber die Metaphysik bringt das Sein selbst nicht zur Sprache, weil sie das Sein nicht in seiner Wahrheit und die Wahrheit nicht als die Unverborgenheit und diese nicht in ihrem Wesen bedenkt. Das Wesen der Wahrheit erscheint der Metaphysik immer nur in der schon abkunftigen Gestalt der Wahrheit der Erkenntnis und der Aussage dieser." (WM, pp. 10-11.) See also WG, p. 12-13; WW, pp. 11-12, 15, 16, 17, 25; N, II, p. 74; SZ, pp. 22-24, 153-154, 218-219, 223-226.

[62] N, II, p. 351.

[63] "Die Metaphysik denkt, insofern sie stets nur das Seiende als das Seiende vorstellt, nicht an das Sein selbst." (WM, p. 8.) See also N, II, p. 350.

is it an accidental, or even a necessary property of Being.[64] Rather, it is that internal energy, if we might so express it, by which beings are at all. It is because of this that beings can be lighted up and appear. Without a prior comprehension of Being we would not be able to experience the beings which are our constant concern.[65] But although this prior grasp of Being is absolutely necessary as the ground of our experience of beings, and although it is the fundamental presupposition of any further knowledge,[66] it remains most obscure. And so for metaphysics the most basic of differences, the ontological difference,[67] that is, the difference between Being and beings, remains forgotten. And further, not only is the difference forgotten, but the forgetfulness is itself forgotten.[68]

The forgottenness of the difference as such which must be thought of here is the veiling which is thought from the standpoint of λήθη (concealment). And on the side of the veiling itself, it withdraws itself primordially. The forgetfulness belongs to the difference because the difference belongs to the forgetfulness.[69]

But because metaphysics, of necessity, must continually speak of beings, and because it gives the appearance of asking after the sense of Being, while it is really only concerned with beings, it has from its beginning to end fostered the confusion between Being and beings, consequent upon the oblivion of the ontological difference between them.

---

[64] As Heinrich Ott points out in this connection: "Sein ist wohl kein selbständiges Etwas, aber es ist etwas 'am Seienden,' an allem Seienden. Und nun nicht nur etwas im Sinne einer zufälligen oder auch notwendigen 'Eigenschaft,' sondern dasjenige, was das Seiende allererst zum Seienden macht: eben das Sein ..." (*Denken und Sein* (Zollikon: Evangelischer Verlag, 1959), p. 130.)

[65] Concerning the necessity of a pre-ontological grasp of Being Eugen Fink remarks: "Sein wird immer im vorhinein verstanden, und dieses Vorverständnis öffnet allererst den Raum für die Begegnung von Seiendem in der Erfahrung. Sein gibt es für uns nicht, weil wir seiende Dinge kennenlernen, sondern wir können nur seiende Dinge kennenlernen, bestimmen, weil wir schon dergleichen wie Sein verstehen." ("Philosophie als Überwindung der Naivität," *Lexis*, I (1948), 116.)

[66] Thus Ott notes: "... ist das Sein die Voraussetzung dafür, dass Seiendes als *Seiendes* gedacht werden kann." (*Denken und Sein* ..., p. 132.)

[67] Concerning the fundamental character of the difference Fink remarks: "Dieser Unterschied ist der ursprünglichste Unterschied überhaupt ..." ("Philosophie als ...," p. 115.)

[68] EM, p. 15. Cf. also WW, pp. 19, 23; HW, p. 244.

[69] "Die hier zu denkende Vergessenheit ist die von der λήθη (Verbergung) her gedachte Verhüllung der Differenz als solche, welche Verhüllung ihrerseits sich anfänglich entzogen hat. Die Vergessenheit gehört zur Differenz, weil diese jener zugehört." (ID, pp. 46-47.)

Metaphysics itself gives the impression, and confirms it, that the question concerning Being is raised and answered. But metaphysics in no way answers the question of the truth of Being, because it never asks this question ... It speaks about Being and means a being as a being. The assertions of metaphysics from its beginning to its consummation have given rise in a strange way to a thoroughgoing confusion of being and a being.[70]

Since it considers a being rather than Being as truth, and since it is completely oblivious of the difference between Being and beings, it is condemned by its very nature to *Seinsvergessenheit*, which is precisely the forgetfulness of the ontological difference.

The forgetfulness of Being is the forgetfulness of the difference between Being and a being.[71]

For this reason in SZ Heidegger attempted to make a new start in ontology, to seek for a new foundation.[72] The old metaphysics, Heidegger contends, had been based on the ὄν ᾗ ὄν, beings as beings. The task that Heidegger addressed himself to in seeking a new foundation in ontology was to attempt to recover what had been forgotten in the ὄν.[73] As long as metaphysics thinks only of beings, ὄν, ὄντα, and not of the truth of Being, it is without a foundation. Thus the attempt to seek the *Sinn von Sein*, or to think through to the truth of Being, is an

---

[70] "Sie selbst erweckt und befestigt den Anschein, als sei durch sie die Frage nach dem Sein gefragt und beantwortet. Allein die Metaphysik antwortet nirgends auf die Frage nach der Wahrheit des Seins, weil sie diese Frage nie fragt. Sie fragt nicht, weil sie das Sein nur denkt, indem sie das Seiende als das Seiende vorstellt ... Sie nennt das Sein und meint das Seiende als Seiende. Das Aussagen der Metaphysik bewegt sich von ihrem Beginn bis in ihre Vollendung auf eine seltsame Weise in einer durchgängigen Verwechslung von Seienden und Sein." (WM, p. 11.)

[71] "Die Seinsvergessenheit ist die Vergessenheit des Unterschieds des Seins zum Seienden." (HW, p. 336.)

[72] After 1929 the word "ontology" is no longer used by Heidegger. In the Introduction to WM, p. 21, which was added in 1949, Heidegger writes that the reason for dropping this term was that it led too easily to a misunderstanding of what he was attempting to do. His work, as he saw it, was not just to do a "deeper" ontology in the traditional sense which would remain within the same perspectives as the traditional ontology, differing from it only by degree. One of Heidegger's perennial difficulties has been, he believes, that his thought has been understood within the language of Western metaphysics, which means, of course, to misunderstand it completely, as he points out in his letter to Richardson. (*Through Phenomenology to Thought* ..., p. VIII and pp. 14-15 on the dropping of the term "ontology".)

[73] WM, p. 20.

attempt to "found" ontology on a new base and hence was called *Fundamentalontologie.*[74]

As long as the truth of Being is not thought all ontology remains without its foundation. Therefore the thinking which in SZ attempted to think forward to the truth of Being was designated as Fundamental Ontology.[75]

But what does this have to do with the logic problematic? We have undertaken this investigation of Heidegger's position on metaphysics and the forgetfulness of Being and its relation to Heidegger's attempt to "found" ontology in SZ because without this wider perspective of *Seins-vergessenheit* and the consequent necessity of a foundational ontology, it would be impossible to understand why Heidegger should take the position that he does with respect to the foundation of the proposition which is central to the work of logic and also the foundation of symbolic logic, which we shall consider in subsequent chapters.

[74] As Birault points out, this new foundation will be the truth of Being: "Ni l'homme, ni la Raison, ni le Monde, ni Dieu ne sont ici considérés comme premier fondement et comme objet ultime de l'interrogation, mais bien ce que Heidegger appelle l'Être et la Lumière ou la Vérité de l'Être." ("Existence et vérité d'après Heidegger," *Revue de Métaphysique et de Morale*, LVI (1950), 39). See also Dondeyne, "La différence ...," p. 56; Richardson, "Heidegger and the Origin of Language," *International Philosophical Quarterly*, II (1962), 404.

[75] "Solange jedoch die Wahrheit des Seins nicht gedacht ist, bleibt alle Ontologie ohne ihr Fundament. Deshalb bezeichnete sich das Denken, das mit 'S. u. Z.' in die Wahrheit des Seins vorzudenken versuchte, als Fundamentalontologie." (HB, p. 41.)

CHAPTER II

THE FOUNDATION AND LIMITATION OF LOGIC

The basic thrust of Heidegger's thought, at least since SZ, has been an implacable struggle against the subject-object dichotomy which was introduced by Descartes.[1] Descartes' thought, however, as seen by Heidegger, is itself simply a variation on a theme which has run through the history of Western metaphysics since Plato.[2] For it was with Plato that the truth of Being, which had been experienced by his Greek forerunners as ἀλήθεια, revelation-concealment,[3] became transformed to ἰδέα.[4] Consequent upon this transmutation, λόγος, φύσις, and νοεῖν which had been inseparably bound to Being, ἐὸν ἔμμεναι,[5] were severed from it.[6] Now, cut off from their life-giving source in Being, and separated from each other, they quickly degenerated into instruments, ὄργανα, to serve man's purposes. Truth is no longer experienced as Being's self-revelation but is reduced to what is expressed in the assertion,[7] which in its turn becomes a tool[8] for the elaboration of science,[9]

---

[1] Johannes Hollenbach, S. J., *Sein und Gewissen* (Baden-Baden: Grimm, 1954), p. 22. See especially the excellent study by Paul Ricœur on the meaning and scope of Heidegger's critique of the subject-ism of Descartes in the essay "The Critique of Subjectivity and the Cogito in the Philosophy of Heidegger," contained in, *Heidegger and the Quest for Truth*, ed. with Introduction by Manfred Frings (Chicago: Quadrangle Books, 1968), pp. 62-75.

[2] HW, pp. 84, 91; PL, pp. 44-46; SZ, pp. 21-26; EM, pp. 143-144.

[3] SZ, pp. 219-220; PL, pp. 32-33; VA, p. 19; HW, pp. 43, 49.

[4] EM, p. 92; PL, pp. 34-35, 41, 42, 46. Cf. also Gerhard Kruger, "Martin Heidegger und der Humanismus," *Studia Philosophica*, IX (1949), 93-94.

[5] WD, p. 139.

[6] On this point see especially the admirable study of George Seidel, O. S. B., *Martin Heidegger and the Presocratics* (Lincoln: U. of Nebraska Press, 1964), pp. 43-49.

[7] EM, p. 130; WD, p. 172.

[8] EM, p. 143.

[9] WD, p. 10. On the relation of symbolic logic to the development of science see the excellent essay of Albert Borgmann, "Heidegger and Symbolic Logic" in *Heidegger and the Quest for Truth* ..., pp. 139-162.

which will henceforth direct itself to the exploitation of nature,[10] now no longer seen as the overpowering emerging-into-presence, but rather as a field to be subdued and controlled. Thought, νοεῖν, sundered from its vital union with Being[11] becomes "*organized*,"[12] until the final culmination is reached in our own days with "thinking" machines.[13] Language, originally identified with λόγος, deteriorates to a mere communications means.[14] And as the final piece of irony, man himself becomes an instrument in a massive, highly "*organized*" society,[15] which has produced an ambience which is so inhuman that he must somehow or other be saved, it is to be hoped, by a new doctrine of humanism,[16] adventitiously applied.

Looked at from a different angle, the transformation of truth to ἰδέα, the consequence of which is the location of truth in the proposition, has ended in the system of Hegel,[17] in which knowledge is made absolute and simultaneously destroyed. Thus Hegel draws out the innermost tendencies of a tradition which situates truth in the proposition and regards the proposition as an instrument in the acquisition of knowledge. By accepting its fundamental starting point, and developing it to its uttermost limit,[18] Hegel shows, without intending to, the complete bankruptcy of a tradition which makes the proposition the locus of truth. He destroys the system from within. Only a short wait is required before Nietzsche's nihilism, also the intellectual progeny of Plato,[19] will destroy it from without[20] by declaring the death of the God which the tradition had attempted to utilize as its supreme grounding.[21]

The consequence of all of this is that man and his metaphysics have arrived at a cul-de-sac. We have seen that in SZ an attempt was made

[10] VA, p. 72; ID, p. 48; EM, pp. 147-148.

[11] N, I, p. 528.

[12] KTS, pp. 34-35.

[13] HH, p. 27.

[14] WD, pp. 99, 168; HW, p. 60; VA, pp. 146, 190, 245; US, pp. 263-264.

[15] HW, p. 81.

[16] For a detailed analysis of what Heidegger understands by "humanism" and his reasons for rejecting it, together with a critical evaluation of his position see Stelios Castanos De Médicis, *Réponse à Heidegger sur l'humanisme* (Paris: Pedone, 1966).

[17] EM, pp. 137-138, 144; WD, p. 146; SG, pp. 145-146.

[18] Bertrand Rioux, *L'Être et la vérité chez Heidegger et S. Thomas d'Aquin* (Paris: Presses Universitaires de France, 1963), p. 111.

[19] Heidegger calls Nietzsche "... der zügelloseste Platoniker innerhalb der Geschichte der abendländischen Metaphysik ..." (PL, p. 37.)

[20] Rioux, *L'Être et la Vérité* ..., p. 111-112.

[21] ID, p. 69.

to seek a new foundation for ontology which would recall the truth of Being. In the interrogation of Being, however, there is one being which is uniquely fitted to give access to Being — man, or better, Dasein, that being which is the "There" (*Da*) of Being (*Sein*).[22]

Since the time of Descartes man has been regarded as a subject.[23] Descartes, as is well known, had sought for an indubitable foundation upon which to erect his philosophic structure, the *fundamentum inconcussum veritatis*.[24] He had found this in the "cogito sum". But as a consequence man is conceived purely from the perspective of subjectivity. He is primarily a *res cogitans*,[25] a thinking thing, who as subject stands apart from a world now composed of objects which are his diametric opposites — *res extensae*.[26] Heidegger, as we mentioned earlier, has been locked in a life and death struggle against this conception of man.[27] In his opinion no remedy such as humanism or a revamped anthropology[28] applied to man *ab extra* can ever be adequate to the amelioration of the situation in which contemporary man finds himself. He must so conceive of himself and his relationship to his world that he will find an appropriate dwelling place.[29] For this reason Heidegger attempts to re-think the nature of man[30] from the standpoint of his involvement in Being.

The essence and the manner of human-being can only be determined from the essence of Being.[31]

To characterize this involvement the term Da-sein was chosen. Da-sein is the "There" of Being, the scene of disclosure, openness to Being.[32]

---

[22] SZ, pp. 7, 8, 37, 314.

[23] SZ, pp. 22, 45-46; HW, pp. 91-92. Cf. also William Richardson, S. J., "Kant and the Later Heidegger," *Phenomenology In America*, (Chicago: Quadrangle Books, 1967), p. 132.

[24] SZ, p. 24.

[25] SZ, pp. 24, 25.

[26] SZ, pp. 66, 89-101.

[27] Werner Marx, "Heidegger's New Conception of Philosophy: The Second Phase of Existentialism," *Social Research*, XXII (1955), 451-474.

[28] Heidegger makes this point clear in a lecture given during the winter semester 1937-38. The fundamental perspective from which man must be viewed is in his relation to Being. This is contained in his letter to Richardson, *Through Phenomenology* ..., p. XXI.

[29] HB, p. 19.

[30] SZ, pp. 196-197.

[31] "Das Wesen und die Weise des Menschseins kann sich dann aber nur aus dem Wesen des Seins bestimmen." (EM, p. 106.)

[32] SZ, p. 12; HB, pp. 15, 24, 35.

To break away from the Cartesian tradition which had split man off from his world, he is also designated as being-in-the-World, *In-der-Welt-sein*.[33]

It will be recalled that the analysis of Dasein undertaken in SZ yielded the result of laying bare the fundamental existential structure of Dasein. This existential structure of Dasein as *In-der-Welt-sein* (to-be-in-the-World) is constituted by three structural moments: *Befindlichkeit* (disposition),[34] *Verstehen* (comprehension),[35] and *Rede* (speech).[36] It is in virtue of this fundamental ontological structure that Dasein as *In-der-Welt-sein* is openness-to (*Erschlossenheit*) the World. In *Befindlichkeit* Dasein's immediate openness to the World is revealed. In *Verstehen* Dasein comprehends Being and the World as the total relational complex of meaningfulness. What is grasped in primordial comprehension (*Verstehen*) by Dasein is appropriated to itself through interpretation (*Auslegung*).

In it (i.e. interpretation) comprehension appropriates to itself that which is comprehended in a comprehending manner. In interpretation comprehension does not become other, but rather it becomes itself. Interpretation is existentially grounded in comprehension, and comprehension does not arise from interpretation. Interpretation is not an acquiring of information about what is comprehended, but the working-out of the possibilities projected in comprehension.[37]

Interpretation is contrasted with assertion or proposition (*Aussage*) which is seen to be of a derivative character.[38] Assertion is only possible if something has already been grasped in comprehension.

The pointing out of the assertion is accomplished on the basis of what has already been disclosed in comprehension.[39]

This is a point to which we shall return very shortly. But first let us complete our brief consideration of Dasein's existential structure. Equipri-

---

[33] SZ, pp. 63-89, 102-130, 350-367.

[34] SZ, sect. 29.

[35] SZ, sect. 31.

[36] SZ, sect. 34.

[37] "In ihr eignet sich das Verstehen sein Verstandenes verstehend zu. In der Auslegung wird das Verstehen nicht etwas anderes, sondern es selbst. Auslegung gründet existenzial im Verstehen, und nicht entsteht dieses durch jene. Die Auslegung ist nicht die Kenntnisnahme des Verstandenen, sondern die Ausarbeitung der im Verstehen entworfenen Möglichkeiten." (SZ, p. 148.)

[38] SZ, p. 160.

[39] "Das Aufzeigen der Aussage vollzieht sich auf dem Grunde des im Verstehen schon Erschlossenen ..." (SZ, p. 156.)

mordial with *Befindlichkeit* and *Verstehen* is the third structural moment of the existential triad, *Rede* (speech, λόγος).[40] "Λόγος is existentially equiprimordial with *Befindlichkeit* and *Verstehen*."[41] It is not to be thought of as something which is tacked on to the analysis as an after-thought. "Therefore it lies at the base of interpretation and assertion."[42] Λόγος is not something which is merely supplementary to interpretation and assertion, so that first we have a thought and only afterwards express it linguistically. That which *can* be articulated (*Artikulierbare*) through λόγος is sense (*Sinn*). That which actually is articulated in speech is called the totality of meaningfulness (*Bedeutungsganze*).[43] Therefore meaning (*Bedeutung*) which is articulated in speech has sense (*Sinn*),[44] since after actual articulation what was only a possibility, that is *Sinn*, is now concretized in the words of our language. The intelligibility of Dasein is articulated into language.[45] That which is articulated in language expresses the totality of meaningfulness.[46] It is not the word-things (*Wörterdinge*) of actual language which are the source of meaning.[47] It is rather the other way around: Dasein has sense (*Sinn*);[48] this sense can be articulated, and through λόγος is in fact

---

[40] SZ, pp. 32, 160-161. The German term *Rede* can be rendered into English as "speech," "discourse," "language," etc. What Heidegger has in mind here, however, is not merely language as spoken, but rather an existential component of Dasein by which Dasein is capable of articulating its meaningfulness. The translation of *Rede* by the Greek λόγος seems to communicate this notion more adequately, and, as Richardson has pointed out, it offers an additional advantage: "It is with *Rede* that Heidegger translates the Greek λόγος. Good English usage permits simple transliteration of the Greek. Since the word assumes an ever increasing importance through the whole evolution of Heidegger, let us use "logos" from the beginning so that we may see the later development in its initial stages." (*Through Phenomenology* ..., p. 66.)

[41] "Die Rede ist mit Befindlichkeit und Verstehen existenzial gleichursprünglich." (SZ, p. 161.)

[42] "Sie liegt daher der Auslegung und Aussage schon zugrunde." (SZ, p. 161.)

[43] "Das in der Auslegung, ursprünglicher mithin schon in der Rede Artikulierbare nannten wir den Sinn. Das in der redenden Artikulation Gegliederte als solches nennen wir das Bedeutungsganze." (SZ, p. 161.)

[44] "Bedeutungen sind als das Artikulierte des Artikulierbaren immer sinnhaft." (SZ, p. 161.)

[45] "Rede ist die Artikulation der Verständlichkeit ... Die Hinausgesprochenheit der Rede ist die Sprache." (SZ, p. 161.)

[46] "Das in der redenden Artikulation Gegliederte als solches nennen wir das Bedeutungsganze ... Das Bedeutungsganze der Verständlichkeit *kommt zu Wort*." (SZ, p. 161.) Heidegger's emphasis.

[47] SZ, p. 161.

[48] SZ, p. 151.

articulated. That which is articulated finds its expression in language which has meaning (*Bedeutung*). At the base of meaning is the fact that Dasein as *In-der-Welt-sein* is open and has the power to articulate its own basic intelligibility, in meaningful language.[49]

According to its authentic possibilities, Dasein's essence is to exist,[50] to stand in the openness of Being,[51] to be the clearing of Being.[52] But in fact, since the time of the early Greeks, man had been defined as the rational animal.[53] This definition, according to Heidegger, is not incorrect, but it is totally inadequate.

... The Greeks ... in the pre-philosophic as well as in the philosophic Dasein interpretation defined the essence of man as ζῷον λόγον ἔχον. The later interpretation of this definition of man in the sense of animal rationale, rational living being, is indeed not false, but it covers up the phenomenal foundation from which this definition of Dasein is taken.[54]

It defines man in terms of *animalitas* rather than by the prerogative which is uniquely his — his comprehension of Being.[55]

The characteristic feature of the Dasein which man is, is determined through the comprehension of Being.[56]

It is this comprehension of Being (*Seinsverständnis*) which constitutes Dasein's ontological structure.

... the comprehension of Being, in which we always antecedently move, *belongs in the final analysis to the essential constitution of Dasein itself.*[57]

---

[49] SZ, p. 161.

[50] SZ, pp. 13, 142, 314. See also KM, pp. 205, 207-221; WW, p. 25; WM, pp. 14-16; HB, p. 14, 15, 16, 25, 31, 35.

[51] ID, p. 22.

[52] HB, p. 15. See also, HB, pp. 25, 45; WM, p. 49; SG, pp. 146, 147.

[53] SZ, p. 25.

[54] "... die Griechen ... in der vorphilosophischen sowohl wie in der philosophischen Daseinsauslegung das Wesen des Menschen bestimmten als ζῷον λόγον ἔχον. Die spätere Auslegung dieser Definition des Menschen im Sinne von animal rationale, 'vernünftiges Lebewesen', ist zwar nicht 'falsch,' aber sie verdeckt den phänomenalen Boden, dem diese Definition des Daseins entnommen ist." (SZ, p. 165.) Cf. also SZ, p. 48; HB, pp. 12, 13, 19, 21-22; VA, pp. 72-74, 91, 94-95; SG, pp. 79, 126, 147, 210; WD, pp. 24-28, 30, 66, 95-96; ID, p. 24; HW, pp. 60-61; EM, pp. 108, 134.

[55] On this point see especially De Médicis, *Réponse à Heidegger sur l'humanisme* ..., p. 29.

[56] "Der Grundzug des Daseins, das der Mensch ist, wird durch das Seinsverständnis bestimmt." (SG, p. 146.)

[57] "... Seinsverständnis, in dem wir uns immer schon bewegen, *und das am Ende zur Wesensverfassung des Daseins selbst gehört.*" (SZ, p. 8.)

It is this which is the foundation of all further knowledge.[58] Even the most casual dealings with beings must somehow presuppose that we have grasped what Being is, else we would not know that they *are*.

... we move always within an antecedent comprehension of Being ... We do not *know* what Being means. But already when we ask: "What *is* 'Being'" we hold ourselves within a comprehension of the "is", although we cannot conceptually fix what "is" means.[59]

This first comprehension of Being, however, is vague and undetermined;[60] it is not grasped by a concept.[61] Somehow man has a pre-ontological comprehension of Being[62] which, though vague, is still an indisputable fact.[63] By "pre-ontological" Heidegger means that while Being has been comprehended, it has not yet been made the theme of an ontological investigation. But this pre-ontological grasp of Being is implied in every statement, even in every word we utter.[64] It is not, however, for all of its primordiality grasped in a clear concept. And this is as it must be, for if it were so grasped, it would then be *a* being, not Being itself.[65]

But what will all of this mean in terms of the logic problematic in general, and the foundation of the proposition in particular? As we noted above, according to Heidegger's interpretation of the history of Western metaphysics a turning point took place in Plato when truth, which had been originally experienced as ἀλήθεια, simultaneous revelation and concealment, changed to ἰδέα, something to be looked at. This changed conception of truth developed through Aristotle and into the middle ages and found its expression in the well-known definition of truth: "Veritas est adaequatio intellectus et rei."[66] Truth is now seen as conformity of thought with thing, its seat is the assertion or proposition.[67]

---

[58] SZ, p. 333.

[59] "... wir bewegen uns immer schon in einem Seinsverständnis ... Wir *wissen* nicht, was 'Sein' besagt. Aber schon wenn wir fragen: 'was *ist* 'Sein?' halten wir uns in einem Verständnis des 'ist' ohne dass wir begrifflich fixieren könnten, was das 'ist' bedeutet." (SZ, p. 5.) See especially SZ, p. 4; and also SZ, pp. 6, 7, 51, 152; KM, pp. 204-205.

[60] SZ, p. 5.

[61] SZ, pp. 4, 8, 315.

[62] SZ, p. 197. See also SZ, pp. 15, 150, 196, 197, 314.

[63] "*Dieses durchschnittliche und vage Seinsverständnis ist ein Faktum.*" (SZ, p. 5.) Heidegger's emphasis.

[64] SZ, pp. 6-7; EM, p. 62; KM, p. 205. See also Fridolin Wiplinger, *Wahrheit und Geschichtlichkeit* (Freiburg/München: Alber, 1961), p. 151.

[65] SZ, pp. 4, 5, 6; EM, p. 67.

[66] SZ, pp. 214-215.

[67] SZ, pp. 33, 54, 214.

For Heidegger, however, this is not the deepest sense of truth. He asks more fundamentally what makes conformity itself possible.[68] In order that the proposition conform to the thing, the thing itself must be opened up for Dasein, must be able to appear and manifest itself. The basis of all truth is openness.[69] Before one can make assertions about things, the thing must be opened to the one who is making the assertion, and he must be open to it.

The correctness of the assertion is only possible because of the openness of comportment...[70]

The truth of the assertion therefore is derivative, inasmuch as it rests upon a more primordial base, that is, the disclosedness (*Entdecktheit*)[71] of the beings which Dasein encounters in its ontic comportment. If beings were not somehow opened up and uncovered to Dasein their truth could not be known and then expressed in the assertion.[72] But in order for beings to be uncovered, and so to manifest themselves for what they are in Dasein's ontic comportment with them, Dasein must have an antecedent comprehension of Being.[73] Dasein, of course, exists in both dimensions, that is, the ontic and the ontological simultaneously, but the antecedent grasp of Being is structurally prior. But although the ontological dimension is structurally prior to the ontic, it is not disclosed (*erschlossen*) until after some instrumental complex has been discovered (*entdeckt*) on the ontic level. In terms of the proposition or assertion problematic this will mean that in Heidegger's view there are three types of truth: the truth of Being (*ontologische Wahrheit*), the truth of beings or ontic truth (*ontische Wahrheit*), and, as a derivative mode, propositional truth (*Satzwahrheit*).[74]

From this it is clear that the proposition has only a limited, if not wholly derivative significance. In section # 33 of SZ where Heidegger examines the meaning and cognitive significance of the proposition he takes as his point of departure Aristotle's definition of the proposition

---

[68] WW, pp. 10-12.

[69] SZ, p. 220; WG, p. 13.

[70] "... nur durch diese Offenständigkeit des Verhaltens die Richtigkeit (Wahrheit) der Aussage möglich wird ... (WW, p. 12).

[71] WG, p. 13.

[72] SZ, p. 218.

[73] SZ, pp. 85-86.

[74] WG, pp. 12-13.

as *apophansis*, a pointing out that lets something be seen.[75] It shows
something *as* something.[76] It is in this letting something be seen as
something that the synthetic character of the assertion is founded.[77]
But in the course of history the synthetic aspect of the proposition
has forced itself so much to the fore that one no longer asks for
the ontological meaning of the proposition.[78] The ontological interpretation which Heidegger undertakes cannot simply take the proposition
for granted, but must attempt to get to its foundation. In the proposition
as apophantic the being about which the predications are made is turned
into an object to which predicates correspond.[79] Beings, when viewed
from this perspective, are seen only as objects which are available or
on hand (*Vorhandene*).

The being which has been grasped pre-ontologically, the hammer for example,
is, in the first instance, ready-to-hand as a tool. If this being becomes the object
of an assertion, then what has been grasped pre-ontologically is transformed in
advance by the stance toward being which the assertion assumes. The *ready-to-hand*
being *with which* we deal and have to do becomes the "being over-which" of
the assertion's pointing out. Our antecedent way of looking at things is aimed

---

[75] SZ, pp. 32-33, 154, 218-219. Heidegger's interpretation of the assertion of course
is not without its critics. Ernst Tugendhat for example critically examines Heidegger's
interpretation of the assertion in relation to that of Husserl at length. See especially,
Der Wahrheitsbegriff bei Husserl und Heidegger (Berlin: De Gruyter, 1967), pp. 331-348.
He finds an ambiguity in Heidegger's use of "Entdecken" (p. 333). This ambiguity creeps in,
so Tugendhat feels, because Heidegger regards the phrase, "wie es an ihm selbst ist"
which is given in the first formulation of the assertion as dispensable (pp. 332-335).
Heidegger's formulation then becomes: "*Wahrsein* (*Wahrheit*) der Aussage muss verstanden
werden als *entdeckend-sein*." (SZ, pp. 218.) We cannot enter into a detailed analysis of
Tugendhat's criticism here, since an examination of Heidegger's position in relation to
Husserl is beyond the scope of the present work. We might note, however, that Heidegger
has arrived at the last mentioned formulation of the assertion because of one of his
principal concerns, truth as ἀλήθεια. As we have noted, he finds the conception of truth
as correspondence inadequate and hence attempts to conceive it in a new way. For this
reason he can no longer be satisfied with the old formulation of truth as correspondence.
It is also for this reason that the phrase 'wie es in ihm selbst ist" is dropped, and
the truth of the assertion is understood as *entdeckend-sein*. This is, of course, related
to another basic concern of SZ, i.e. the attempt to overcome the subject-object dichotomy.
Thus Heidegger adds, immediately after he has come to the new formulation mentioned
above: "Wahrheit hat also gar nicht die Struktur einer Übereinstimmung zwischen
Erkennen und Gegenstand im Sinne einer Angleichung eines Seienden (Subjekt) an ein
anderes (Objekt)." (SZ, pp. 218-219.)

[76] SZ, pp. 33, 158.

[77] SZ, pp. 33, 154-155, 159.

[78] SZ, p. 160.

[79] SZ, pp. 155, 158, 224.

at a being present-at-hand in a being-ready-to-hand. The ready-to-hand as ready-to-hand becomes veiled both through this stance of looking-at, and for the sake of it.[80]

But Dasein's world is not a simple panorama of objects viewed from the distance of disinterestedness. The world is, rather, a network of things which are interrelated with one another, and this interrelatedness comes about because the things (*Zuhandene*) of the world are involved in Dasein's projects.[81]

We are now in a position to consider in greater detail a distinction which is introduced by Heidegger in SZ, the understanding of which is essential to the logic problematic. Heidegger distinguishes between two "as" structures (*Als-Struktur*), the apophantic "as" of the assertion which lets something be seen as something,[82] and the hermeneutic "as" of interpretation which is proper to our concernful dealings with beings.

Thus assertion cannot disavow its ontological origin from comprehending interpretation. The primordial "as" of circumspective comprehending interpretation (ἑρμηνεία) we name the existential-hermeneutical "as" in distinction to the *apophantic* "as" of assertion.[83]

The hermeneutic "as" of our practical concern takes something in a way in which it is related to man's interests and concerns. The thing is not merely something which is looked at or observed, something available (*Vorhandenes*). It is related to man through being involved in his plans and projects. The well-known example which Heidegger employs to illustrate this is the hammer.[84] The hammer which Dasein uses circumspectively is not merely present-at-hand (*Vorhandenes*). It is a tool which is directed to a certain piece of work, the making of shoes, desks, or whatever.[85] It has a purpose and because it is suited to help Dasein

[80] "Das in der Vorhabe gehaltene Seiende, der Hammer zum Beispiel, ist zunächst zuhanden als Zeug. Wird dieses Seiende 'Gegenstand' einer Aussage, dann vollzieht sich mit dem Aussageansatz im vorhinein ein Umschlag in der Vorhabe. Das *zuhandene Womit* des Zutunhabens, der Verrichtung, wird zum '*Worüber*' der aufzeigenden Aussage. Die Vorsicht zielt auf ein Vorhandenes am Zuhandenen. *Durch* die Hin-sicht und *für* sie wird das Zuhandene als Zuhandenes verhüllt." (SZ, pp. 157-158.) Heidegger's emphasis.

[81] SZ, p. 84-88, 148-151.

[82] SZ, pp. 33, 158.

[83] "So kann die Aussage ihre ontologische Herkunft aus der verstehenden Auslegung nicht verleugnen. Das ursprüngliche 'Als' der umsichtig verstehenden Auslegung (ἑρμηνεία) nennen wir das existenzial-*hermeneutische* 'Als' im Unterschied vom *apophantischen* 'Als' der Aussage." (SZ, p. 158.) Heidegger's emphasis.

[84] SZ, p. 69.

[85] SZ, p. 84.

achieve the purpose for which he employs it, it refers to something, e.g. a shoe or desk.[86] It stands within a definite context of meaningful relations,[87] e.g. hammer to nail, nail to shoe, and shoe is related to Dasein as its ultimate "for-the-sake-of-which (*Worum-willen*).[88] In this scheme of things beings-ready-to-hand (*Zuhandene*) stand within a total relational complexus in which they are related to each other and ultimately to Dasein as their final "for-the-sake-of-which" (*Worum-willen*). The whole matrix of relations, destinations, and meanings, the world as the environmental world (*Umwelt*) of our everyday life, is referred to Dasein as its ultimate "for-the-sake-of-which" (*Worum-willen*). This relational totality is projected by Dasein through his purposes, goals, and enterprises.

Of the two "as" structures, the apophantic "as" structure of assertion and the hermeneutic "as" structure of comprehension it is the latter which is the more primordial, the former which is derivative,[89] since it is through the existential-hermeneutical "as" of concernful understanding that beings are opened up in their Being.[90] These beings which have become part of Dasein's projects are not simply *Vorhandene*, available things, things to be looked at, the objects of theoretical (θεωρεῖν, to view) science.[91] They are, rather, opened up to Dasein through concernful dealing with them. And Dasein, by its very ontological structure, is openness to Being; it has a primordial comprehension of Being. Without this grasp of Being there would be no possibility of encountering beings, since in order to know that they *are*, it is necessary to have grasped Being antecedently.

From this it becomes clear that Dasein's structure is circular:[92] prior to being able to formulate the Being-question it must have grasped Being at least in some manner, and this primordial experience of Being enters into the articulation of the question.[93] Dasein's comprehension of Being, then, forms a circle, and the circle is hermeneutical: there is a primordial pre-ontological comprehension of Being; this comprehension of Being is interpreted, but this interpretation itself must already have compre-

---

[86] SZ, p. 84.
[87] SZ, pp. 68, 83-84, 145-151.
[88] SZ, p. 84.
[89] SZ, p. 158.
[90] SZ, pp. 69, 83, 158.
[91] SZ, pp. 68-69, 138, 356-364.
[92] SZ, p. 153.
[93] SZ, p. 8.

hended what is to be interpreted.[94] Every interpretation is grounded
on something which is had in advance. This is achieved by the three
fore-structures of comprehension sc. *Vorhabe* (what is had antecedently),
Vorsicht (what is seen in advance), and *Vorgriff* (anticipatory comprehension).[95] It is because of the fore-structure of comprehension that
something can be encountered *as* something, e.g. house *as* house.[96]
Thus when something such as a house is encountered as a *Zuhandenes*
it is not the case that we meet it first as a *Vorhandenes* which is
merely present and only afterwards tack a meaning on to it *as* something.[97]
When something within-the-World is encountered *as* something in-the-
World it is already uncovered to comprehension in its relational in-
volvements simply by being comprehended as being-in-the-World, and
it is the relational involvement which is "laid out" (*Auslegung*), that
is interpreted, in the interpretation.[98]

There is, then, a close structural relationship between the primordial
grasp of Being by comprehension and the hermeneutical "as" structure
of interpretation by which something *as* something is opened up to
Dasein. The reason that the structure of Dasein is circular is because
Dasein is *In-der-Welt-sein*. What Heidegger is attempting to do here
is to overcome the scission of subject and object, and thus he conceives
of man as existing in a profound unity with the truth of Being.[99]
Being is not to be reduced to a product of his reason, a conceptual
representation (*Vorstellung*), or as produced by his activity as a subject.

Comprehension of Being, as here understood, never means that man, as a subject,
possesses a subjective representation of Being, and that Being is merely a representation.[100]

Dasein's nature is to stand in the truth of Being, to be a field of openness
for the clearing of Being — "Comprehension of Being means to say
that man according to his essence stands in the openness of the project
of Being ..."[101] Being addresses a command which is an evocation to

---

[94] SZ, p. 152.
[95] SZ, p. 150.
[96] SZ, p. 149.
[97] SZ, p. 150.
[98] SZ, p. 150.
[99] EM, p. 89.
[100] "Seinsverständnis meint hier niemals, der Mensch besitze als Subjekt eine subjektive
Vorstellung vom Sein und dieses, das Sein, sei eine blosse Vorstellung." (SG, p. 146.)
Cf. also Ott, *Denken und Sein* ..., p. 44.
[101] "Seinsverständnis besagt dass der Mensch seinem Wesen nach im Offenen des
Entwurfes des Seins steht ..." (SG, p. 146.)

authentic thought, to which Dasein responds, or with which he enters into dialogue.

... From ancient times in our history thought has meant: to respond (*entsprechen*) to the hail (*Geheiss*) of Being ...[102]

This is not thought in the sense of a calculation of possible ways of manipulating objects,[103] but rather a letting-be of Being, an allowing of Being to reveal itself.[104] Being needs its "Da" if it is to be lighted up in such a way that it can appear.

But man is pressed into such a manner of being, cast into the need of such Being, because the overpowering as such, in order to appear as prevailing *needs* a place of openness. The essence of human-being only reveals itself to us when it is understood from the standpoint of this need which is the need of Being itself.[105]

Dasein is needed by Being if the voice which Being speaks[106] and which Dasein alone can comprehend, is to be heard and expressed in authentic language which will hold it in openness.[107] Being deputizes Dasein to work, especially through authentic thought, and solicitude for language, on the building of a world that will be a suitable dwelling place for human being.

This dwelling place which man needs is a place in which he can ex-sist. It is a clearing, an open-place, and since he is an ex-sisting being it is a clearing where Being can manifest itself. But Dasein is, as it were, co-sent (*Beschickten*) with Being. Being clears a place for itself through Da-sein. Da-sein is the "there" or the field where, and by which, Being is dis-closed. Dasein is, then, Being's deputy (*Beschickten*), in that Dasein helps bring to pass a clearing for Being. All of these notions are expressed in the very rich text which follows.

As the deputies co-sent (*Beschickten*) by Being in the destining of Being (*Geschick des Seins*) we stand, and indeed according to our essence, in the clearing of Being.

---

[102] "... von altersher besagt in unserer Geschichte Denken so viel wie: dem Geheiss des Seins entsprechen ..." (SG, p. 147.)

[103] G, pp. 14-15; WM, pp. 47-48.

[104] WW, pp. 14, 15, 18; VA, p. 211; WD, p. 123.

[105] "Der Mensch ist aber in ein solches Da-sein genötigt, in die Not solchen Seins geworfen, weil das Überwältigende als ein solches, um waltend zu erscheinen, die Stätte der Offenheit für es *braucht*. Von dieser durch das Sein selbst ernötigten Not her verstanden, eröffnet sich uns erst das Wesen des Menschseins." (EM, p. 124.) Heidegger's emphasis.

[106] N, II, p. 484. Cf. also WM, p. 50; WP, p. 36.

[107] HH, p. 29.

But we do not just stand around idly with no claim on us in this clearing; rather we stand in it as ones claimed by the Being of being. As standers in the clearing of Being we are deputies of Being set into a space freed for temporal activity. This means: we are to build and cultivate the clearing of Being, and this is to be understood in the manifold sense of: to preserve it in trust.[108]

Now, since it is Dasein's nature to stand in the truth of Being and by co-responding to the voice of Being to help to bring to pass the truth of Being which is held in the openness of its disclosure by language, language is the only appropriate abode for man, wherein he, as an existing being, i.e. a being who can grasp Being in its truth, may dwell.

Rather language is the house of Being and only by dwelling in language can man ex-sist since in caring for the truth of Being he also belongs to it.[109]

Being sends itself to Dasein, and in sending itself clears[110] and sets in order the place of its clearing.[111] But if the clearing is to be a clearing it requires a being who can perceive the light of the clearing,[112] and who will protect and care for the clearing. Following Heidegger's own metaphor, it stands in need of forest guardians (*Waldhüter*).[113] According to this conception, man is not the despot of Being but the shepherd

---

[108] "Als die im Geschick des Seins vom Sein Beschickten stehen wir, und zwar unserem Wesen nach, in einer Lichtung des Seins. Aber wir stehen in dieser Lichtung keineswegs unangesprochen herum, sondern stehen in ihr als die vom Sein des Seienden in dessen Anspruch Genommenen. Wir sind als die in der Lichtung des Seins Stehenden die Beschickten, die in den Zeit-Spiel-Raum Eingeräumten. Dies sagt: Wir sind die in diesem Spielraum und für ihn Gebrauchten, gebraucht, an der Lichtung des Seins zu bauen und zu bilden, im weiten vielfältigen Sinne: sie zu verwahren." (SG, p. 146.)

[109] "Vielmehr ist die Sprache das Haus des Seins, darin wohnend der Mensch ek-sistiert, indem er der Wahrheit des Seins, sie hutend, gehört." (HB, pp. 21-22.) Cf. also HH, pp. 19, 25.

[110] HB, p. 25; WM, pp. 14-15.

[111] "Sein schickt sich dem Menschen zu, indem es lichtend dem Seienden als solchem einen Zeit-Spiel-Raum einräumt." (SG, p. 129.) And also on the meaning of Being's sending itself and clearing a place for itself, SG, pp. 108-109: "Denn 'schicken' besagt ursprünglich: bereiten, ordnen, jegliches dorthin bringen, wohin es gehört, daher auch einräumen und einweisen; ein Haus, eine Kammer beschicken heisst: in der rechten Ordnung, eingeräumt und aufgeräumt halten."

[112] Kuhn brings out very well some of the nuances of meaning that should be felt in the word *Lichtung*: "Die Lichtung entsteht dadurch, dass der Wald sich lichtet. Aber nur dadurch, dass ein Lichtempfindendes Wesen auf die Lichtung tritt, wird die Lichtung wirklich eine Lichtung, wird der Wald als Wald sichtbar. Der Mensch ist sowohl die Lichtung selbst als auch die Wahrnehmung des gelichteten." ("Heideggers 'Holzwege' ...," p. 256.)

[113] HW, Prologue.

of Being.[114] He is claimed[115] and needed by Being — "The essence of man is assigned to the truth, because the truth needs man."[116] Without Being's sending itself and clearing for itself a place of manifestation, there would be no revelation of truth, language, or history. Without a being uniquely open to the reception of Being's sending itself and capable of being attuned to its silent voice, and having grasped it, to hold it in openness in language,[117] there would also be no revelation, language, or history. Being and Dasein stand in need of each other.[118] Still, in the sending of itself, in the revelation of itself as truth, the initiative is always Being's.[119]

In this conception of man it can be seen that man has a unique dignity. He is not one entity among many, albeit different from the animal in virtue of his power of *ratio*. Rather he alone of all beings is open to Being, is the place where the truth of Being is revealed,[120] and can comprehend Being in its truth.

... If the comprehension of Being did not come to pass man could not be the being which he is, even though he were fitted out with other powers, however wonderful.[121]

True, he no longer views his relationship to Being, to language, to thought, and to the world in terms of so many instruments of exploitation.[122] From this perspective he is the guardian of Being's clearing,[123] rather than a despotic and sometimes capricious master. He has, to use Heidegger's expression, gained the poverty of the shepherd.[124]

---

[114] "Der Mensch ist nicht der Herr des Seienden. Der Mensch ist der Hirt des Seins." (HB, p. 29.)

[115] N, II, p. 484.

[116] "Das Menschenwesen ist der Wahrheit übereignet, weil die Wahrheit den Menschen braucht." (G, p. 65.)

[117] HW, pp. 60-61.

[118] G, p. 65.

[119] HB, p. 19. Cf. also Ingeborg Koza, *Das Problem des Grundes in Heideggers Auseinandersetzung mit Kant* (Ratingen bei Düsseldorf: A. Henn, 1967), pp. 24-25.

[120] WM, p. 14. Cf. also HB, p. 20; ED, p. 23.

[121] "... geschähe das Verstehen von Sein nicht, der Mensch vermöchte als das Seiende, das er ist, nie zu sein, und wäre er auch mit noch so wunderbarem Vermögen ausgestattet." (KM, p. 205.)

[122] HD, p. 35; WM, p. 49; G, pp. 19-20. Cf. also *The Later Heidegger and Theology*, ed. James Robinson and John Cobb (New York: Harper and Row, 1963), pp. 20, 29.

[123] WD, p. 85. Cf. also EM, p. 108.

[124] HB, p. 29.

From these considerations several conclusions which have importance for the logic problematic have emerged. First, for Heidegger, the concept does not have primacy for Dasein. There is a pre-conceptual, pre-logical (pre-ontological) grasp of Being which is the foundation upon which any further knowledge must be built. Secondly, Being is not determined from thought and the proposition[125] since there is a pre-predicative grasp of truth which is even more fundamental.[126] The assertion or proposition which is the keystone of traditional logic may be one seat of truth[127] but it is certainly not the only one, or even the primary one. The proposition then, from the standpoint of ontological priority is, strictly speaking, derivative.[128] Thirdly, Dasein's comprehension of Being is not the product of its busy activity as a knowing subject. Rather, Being is grasped by a thankful gesture of acceptance[129] and carefully guarded.[130] Fourthly, as a corollary of this, logic is not the first rule of thought;[131] thought is ruled, rather, by its relationship to the command (Geheiss) of Being.[132]

Is thinking of this sort logical? No, surely not, if by the word "logical" we remain within the logico-metaphysical tradition dominant since Plato. Is it "non-rational"? Yes, again if we remain in this tradition. This is, as we shall see, not at all to say that it is "irrational".[133]

---

[125] DF, pp. 35, 137-138.

[126] SZ, p. 149.

[127] DF, p. 122.

[128] SZ, pp. 153-154. See also WW, pp. 12, 15, 16, 17, 25.

[129] For a development of the notion of thinking as "thanksgiving" see the study of Joseph Kockelmans, "Thanks-giving: The Completion of Thought," in Heidegger and the Quest for Truth ..., pp. 163-183.

[130] WM, p. 49; WD, pp. 91-95.

[131] WM, pp. 28, 36-37; EM, pp. 91-93.

[132] HB, p. 47; WD, 99; DF, p. 137.

[133] Richardson, "Heideggers Weg ...," p. 387: "Zugleich ist es nicht-logisch; so lange wir deshalb im Horizont von Logik und Metaphysik bleiben, und d.h. im Horizont des Seienden, können wir Sein nur als Nichts, als Nicht-Seiendes betrachten. Wenn weiter 'rational' (ratio) so viel wie 'logisch' (Logos) meint, dann muss dieses Denken als nicht-rational bezeichnet werden: freilich heisst das ebensowenig irrational wie bloss anti-rational."

CHAPTER III

HEIDEGGER'S "ATTACK" ON LOGIC:
THE NOTHING

As we have seen, Heidegger contends that the history of Western metaphysics has been a record of the forgetfulness of Being. He asserts this because, although metaphysics has treated of being (*das Seiende*) in the sense of the ὄν ᾗ ὄν, it has not grasped Being (*Sein*) as truth-process, that is, as ἀλήθεια. As we shall see in much more detail in the next chapter when we make ἀλήθεια the object of a thematic treatment, ἀλήθεια, at least as Heidegger interprets the history of philosophy, had, for the early Greeks, the sense of simultaneous revelation and concealment. The consideration of Being as truth, that is, simultaneous revelation and concealment, leads us now to a consideration of the Nothing (*das Nichts*), since Being's concealment is due to the fact that Being and the Nothing are inextricably bound together. Further, as we have already seen, Heidegger's constant preoccupation has been to meditate the sense of Being, that is, Being as truth. Indeed, the first page of SZ states that the purpose of the work is to raise anew the question of the sense of Being. As Heidegger's thought unfolds he must also confront the question of the Nothing, as he does for example in WM. That this should be so is clear enough: the depth of our questioning about the Nothing is the measure which will indicate the depth of our questioning about Being itself.[1] And it is in confronting the question of the Nothing in WM that Heidegger's most famous statement on logic, which we have already briefly touched upon, occurs. Thus from the question of the Nothing we will be led to questions which are of fundamental importance to the whole logic problematic.

In the much-quoted inaugural lecture which took place on the occasion of his accession to the chair of philosophy at Freiburg in 1929 Heidegger delivered what is perhaps the best known and most frequently quoted of his statements on logic.

[1] EM, p. 18.

... the Nothing is the source of negation and not the other way around. If this breaks the might of understanding in the field of questioning into the Nothing and Being, then the fate of the dominance of "logic" disintegrates in the whirl of a more primordial questioning.[2]

This inaugural lecture by Heidegger in which he thematized the Nothing and had some rather uncomplimentary things to say about logic and science provoked, as might be expected, a stinging counterattack by the logicians, particularly the logical positivists of the Vienna Circle.[3] Thus Carnap in an article entitled, "Die Überwindung der Metaphysik durch logische Analyse der Sprache," which appeared in *Erkenntnis*, in 1932[4] undertook a critical analysis of this lecture and concluded that it was not only meaningless, but even absurd. We shall see more of Carnap's riposte in a few moments when we take up the question of the primacy of the principle of contradiction in logic.

But let us return to Heidegger's statement. Just how is this statement to be understood? Should it be taken as a total rejection of reason and logic as worthless? What is Heidegger attempting to say in this obviously provocative and polemical statement?[5]

[2] "... das Nichts ist der Ursprung der Verneinung, nicht umgekehrt. Wenn so die Macht des Verstandes im Felde der Fragen nach dem Nichts und dem Sein gebrochen wird, dann entscheidet sich damit auch das Schicksal der Herrschaft der 'Logik' innerhalb der Philosophie. Die Idee der 'Logik' selbst löst sich auf im Wirbel eines ursprünglicheren Fragens." (WM, pp. 36-37.)

[3] Wittgenstein, while never himself a member of the Vienna Circle, was very close to some of its members, particularly Waismann. It is interesting to note that in a conversation with Waismann concerning Heidegger which occurred in the year 1929, shortly after the publication of SZ, at least part of which Wittgenstein had read, Wittgenstein manifests a deep appreciation for the task that Heidegger was attempting, particularly with respect to Being, the Nothing and the analysis of Angst. The whole letter should be read in full. Space permits us to quote only the following:
"Ich kann mir wohl denken, was Heidegger mit Sein und Angst meint. Der Mensch hat den Trieb, gegen die Grenzen der Sprache anzurennen. Denken Sie z.B. an *das Erstaunen, dass etwas existiert*. Das Erstaunen kann nicht in Form einer Frage ausgedruckt werden, und es gibt auch gar keine Antwort. Alles, was wir sagen mögen, kann a priori nur Unsinn sein. Trotzdem rennen wir gegen die Grenze der Sprache an .... Aber die Tendenz, das Anrennen, *deutet auf etwas hin*. Das hat schon der heilige Augustin gewusst, wenn er sagt: Was, du Mistvieh, du willst keinen Unsinn reden? Rede nur einen Unsinn, es macht Nichts!" *Friedrich Waismann: Wittgenstein und der Wiener Kreis*, ed. B. F. Mc Guinness (Oxford: Blackwell, 1967), pp. 68-69.

[4] This article has been translated and is contained in *Logical Positivism*, ed. A. J. Ayer (Glencoe: Free Press, 1960), under the title, "The Elimination of Metaphysics Through Logical Analysis," pp. 60-81.

[5] Otto Pöggeler, *Der Denkweg Martin Heideggers* (Pfullingen: Neske, 1963), p. 273.

The more primordial questioning to which Heidegger makes reference offers a clue as to the way in which this statement is to be understood. The type of questioning that he has in mind is one which again raises the long forgotten question about Being and the Nothing which in this lecture is approached from the Nothing which is inseparably bound to the Being of beings.[6] Logic, one should be careful to note, is placed in quotation marks in this text, and so is used in a special sense. Thus Heidegger in the *Nachwort* to the inaugural lecture which dates from 1943, attempted to dissipate some of the confusion which resulted from the lecture (WM, p. 45) by pointing out that the "logic" which was spoken of was placed in quotes in order to indicate that it is only one way of interpreting thought.

Why was this term placed in quotation marks in this lecture? In order to indicate that this 'logic' is only *one* interpretation of the essence of thought ...[7]

Thus the idea of "logic" "which is dissolved" by a more original manner of questioning is to be understood as a "logic" which totally dominates all philosophic thinking. What is placed into question here is the notion which has been taken for granted throughout the history of Western metaphysics — the unquestioned supremacy of logic as the court of last resort to whose decisions all philosophic thought must be subjected. It is this previously unquestioned supremacy of logic that must now be made questionable.[8] The "more primordial questioning" must now raise the question as to whether the previously unquestioned rule of logic in thought is supreme and whether it alone gives access to the quest after Being. What has also become questionable to this more original way of thinking is whether logic exhausts all of the possibilities of thought. But, one might ask, why should Heidegger single out logic? His reason for this is clear. In doing the Dasein analysis of SZ Heidegger had discovered that one of the richest areas of investigation in his interrogation after the sense of Being was the Angst experience of Dasein. Further the phenomenological analysis of Angst had revealed that this experience was brought about as Dasein encountered his own finitude, or to put it a different way, when Dasein experiences the Nothing. But if the phenomenological investigation into the Nothing has yielded

---

[6] WM, pp. 39-40. Cf. also Pöggeler, *Der Denkweg* ..., p. 273.

[7] "Warum setzt die Vorlesung diesen Titel zwischen Anführungsstriche? Um anzudeuten, dass die 'Logik' nur *eine* Auslegung des Wesens des Denkens ist ..." (WM, p. 47.) My emphasis. See also FM, p. 92 where he makes the same point.

[8] WM, p. 28.

such rich results for the Being-question which is his central concern, then any mode of thought which would reduce the investigation of the Nothing to "nonsense" and "absurdity" could scarcely be countenanced. But, as we have seen, certain logicians, particularly those of the logical positivist persuasion, for example Carnap, did precisely that. It was to a large extent, what Heidegger viewed as their insufferable arrogance, which he was attacking. But we shall see more of this in a few moments. Let us now return to the question of the Nothing.

Being and the Nothing are indissolubly bound together — "es gibt Sein *und Nichts.*" [9] The being which sends itself to Dasein is a revelation that is shrouded in darkness because it is inextricably bound up with the Nothing.

We think the Nothing, insofar as it is bound up with Being itself. We think this "bound up with" itself as history. We think this history as the history of Being itself through which the essencing of this historicity likewise determines itself from out of Being itself. [10]

If Being, in coming to presence, reveals itself, still the veil of non-being is never absent from its self-manifestation. [11] Thus from the beginning of the quest after Being, the quest after the Nothing (*das Nichts*) has gone hand-in-hand with it. In fact the depth of our questioning about the Nothing is the very measure which will indicate the depth of our questioning about Being. [12] This is not surprising, since the ontological difference itself between Being and beings, between beings and what is not-a-being, is the "not". [13] "The ontological difference is the Not between being and Being." [14]

---

[9] ZS, p. 38. My emphasis.

[10] Wir denken das Nichts, insofern es das Sein selbst angeht. Wir denken dieses 'Angehen' selbst als Geschichte. Wir denken diese Geschichte als die Geschichte des Seins selbst, wobei das Wesende dieser Geschichtlichkeit gleichfalls aus dem Sein selbst bestimmt." (N, II, p. 355.)

[11] HW, pp. 39-40; WM, pp. 50-51.

[12] EM, p. 18.

[13] For a more detailed treatment of this point see Alfredo Guzzoni, "Ontologische Differenz und Nichts," contained in, *Martin Heidegger zum siebzigsten Geburtstag: Festschrift* (Pfullingen: Neske, 1959), pp. 35-48. See also Kurt Jürgen Huch who critically examines Heidegger's position and also attempts to relate it historically to nominalism and German idealism, and in particular to Kant and Schelling in, *Philosophiegeschichtliche Voraussetzungen der Heideggerschen Ontologie* (Frankfurt am Main: Europäische Verlagsanstalt, 1967), pp. 21-43.

[14] "Die ontologische Differenz ist das Nichts zwischen Seiendem und Sein." (WG, p. 5.)

But Dasein, as it finds itself in the world, has constantly to do with beings, rather than Being.[15] It becomes, as it were, submerged under the flood of beings.[16] But the more it turns toward beings, the less it is inclined to think of Being.[17] Dasein becomes alienated (*Entfremdung*) from Being,[18] separated from the region which is its true homeland.[19] At the same time, the more Dasein becomes preoccupied with beings, the less it is concerned with what-is-not-a-being (*Nicht-Seiende*).

First of all and for the most part we are blocked from gaining access to the Nothing. By what? Because of the fact that in a certain manner we completely lose ourselves in being. The more we turn ourselves toward being in our hustle and bustle of daily activity, so much the less do we allow being as such to slip away, and so much the more do we turn away from the Nothing.[20]

Dasein becomes homeless (*Heimatlosigkeit*), lost among the welter of beings that engulf it, separated from Being,[21] the remembrance of which is its unique prerogative and destiny.[22] This is the condition which is called *Verfallenheit* in SZ.[23]

As Dasein becomes more and more enthralled with the cultivation of beings it begins to develop the several sciences which have as their singular objective beings, what-is, and nothing else.[24] The sciences as Heidegger sees it, are legitimate and laudable enterprises.[25] They investigate beings and have many interesting and informative things to say about them. With The Nothing, however, they have nothing whatever to do. But in addition to not concerning themselves with The Nothing they attempt to dismiss any question about it with a supercilious air

---

[15] EM, pp. 99-100.

[16] EM, p. 129.

[17] Fink brings this point out very well, noting that: "Er bleibt vom Seienden benommen und hat des Seins vergessen; sein Umgang mit den Dingen sieht nun so aus, als gebe es eben nur Seiendes. Der Unterschied von Sein und Seiendem bleibt als solcher verborgen." ("Philosophie als ...," p. 127.)

[18] SZ, pp. 177-178.

[19] HD, p. 23.

[20] "... das Nichts ist uns zunächst und zumeist in seiner Ursprünglichkeit verstellt. Wodurch denn? Dadurch dass wir uns in bestimmter Weise völlig an das Seiende verlieren. Je mehr wir uns in unseren Umtrieben an das Seiende kehren, um so weniger lassen wir es als solches entgleiten, um so mehr kehren wir uns ab vom Nichts." (WM, pp. 35-36.)

[21] HB, p. 26.

[22] HB, pp. 19, 21-22, 31.

[23] SZ, pp. 114-130, 167-180; HB, p. 21.

[24] WM, pp. 26-27.

[25] ZS, p. 37; WM, p. 13; G, p. 24; DF, pp. 51, 122.

of assumed superiority,[26] as being chimerical and absurd.[27] He who insists that in interrogating Being one must also question about The Nothing does not know what he is doing. Thought must always be thought of something.[28] To think of Nothing is against the very nature of thought. Further, he who insists on speaking of Nothing is involved in a patent violation of the principle of contradiction — either what we are speaking of is being, or it is nothing at all.[29] To speak of the Nothing is thus unwittingly to hypostatize it.[30] When we speak of Nothing we have, *eo ipso*, turned it into something,[31] and hence our discourse contradicts itself. But speech which contradicts itself is meaningless. Thus all talk about The Nothing which is not subjected to logic's principle of contradiction is to be dismissed as puerile nonsense.[32]

Thus Carnap after subjecting the inaugural address, which thematized the Nothing, to a close logical analysis concluded that it is both "meaningless" and "absurd." He remarks:

let us now take a look at some examples of metaphysical pseudo-statements of a kind where the violation of logical syntax is especially obvious, though they accord with historical-grammatical syntax. We select a few sentences from the metaphysical school which at present exerts the strongest influence in Germany ... Sentence II B 2 ("The Nothing nothings") adds something new, viz. the fabrication of the meaningless word "to nothing". This sentence, therefore, is senseless for a twofold reason. We pointed out before that the meaningless words of metaphysics usually owe their origin to the fact that a meaningful word is deprived of its meaning through its metaphorical use in metaphysics. But here we confront one of those rare cases where a new word is introduced which never had a meaning to begin with. Likewise sentence II B 3 ("The Nothing exists only because ...") must be rejected for two reasons. In respect of the error of using the word "nothing" as a noun, it is like the previous sentences. But in addition it involves a contradiction. For even if it were admissible to introduce "nothing" as a name or description of an entity, still the existence of this entity would be denied in its very definition, whereas sentence 3 ("The Nothing exists only because ...") goes on to affirm its existence. This sentence, therefore, would be contradictory, hence absurd, even if it were not already meaningless'.[33]

Here Carnap argues that the famous "the Nothing nothings" (*Das Nichts nichtet*) is syntactic nonsense. In this pseudo-statement "the

[26] WM, p. 40.
[27] EM, p. 20.
[28] WM, p. 28.
[29] EM, pp. 30-31; HB, pp. 33-34.
[30] WM, pp. 27, 30.
[31] N, II, p. 51.
[32] EM, pp. 17-18.
[33] *Logical Positivism* ..., pp. 69-71.

Nothing" is the argument of the functor "nothings". The expression "nothings" is a monadic, statement-generating, name-generating functor. But from the standpoint of syntactics it obviously cannot be name-generating, for syntactically what is "Nothing"? It is evidently not a name. When we say "there is nothing", we are really trying to say, "for every x it is not the case that x is here and now". "Nothing" is therefore an abbreviation for the negation. The negation, however, is not a name but a functor. From the syntactic standpoint it is merely a pseudo-statement, and meaningless.

Does this mean to say, as many have suggested, that the whole fabric of *Was ist Metaphysik* in which "the Nothing" is thematized, rests upon what must be regarded as nonsense? Nonsense, it might be well to note, is of several sorts. If by nonsense we mean syntactic nonsense, then one would be forced to concede that it is nonsense. However, one ought to be quite clear that although a statement may be *syntactic* nonsense, this in no way says that it is semantic nonsense. The two are not at all the same and must be sharply distinguished, something, unfortunately, which was not always done following Carnap's article. Hence although the "Nothing" statements may be syntactic nonsense, this does not at all say that the phenomenological description of dread to which they are related is not something that is perfectly valid, and indeed a very valuable contribution to human thought.

Thus, although science and logic would reject from the start any consideration of The Nothing,[34] it is not at all certain that these are the only approaches to reality. What if logic and its principle of contradiction[35] is not the highest court of appeal in this case?[36]

---

[34] WM, p. 28.

[35] The status of the principle of contradiction and its role in logic has, of course, been critically examined by many modern logicians. It would indeed be an oversimplification of a rather large order to assert that the principle of contradiction is the first law of thought for the logician as Heidegger does (e.g. WM, p. 28). We cannot develop this very complex question concerning the principle of contradiction in any further detail here. For an excellent summary of the recent developments on this much controverted question see P. Gochet, "La Nature du principe de contradiction," *Memorias Del XIII Congreso Internacional De Filosofia*, V (1964), 469-489.

[36] EM, pp. 19-20; WP, pp. 9-11; DF, pp. 78, 80, 92, 122, 137. See especially the excellent study of Karl Heinz Volkmann-Schluck, "Der Satz vom Widerspruch als Anfang der Philosophie," in which he carefully traces out the sense in which the principle of contradiction may be of assistance to authentic thought. It only impedes thought, according to Volkmann-Schluck, when it is taken as the first rule of thought. This study is contained in, *Martin Heidegger zum Siebzigsten Geburtstag* ..., pp. 134-150.

What if science, for whom The Nothing is pure fantasy, is not the supreme standard of all thinking? What if there is a thinking which is even more original than the thinking of science and logic, and what if this thinking can grasp The Nothing and speak meaningfully about it?[37] Such, as a matter of fact, is the case.[38] Both poetic and philosophical thinking[39] can have a primordial *prise de conscience* of The Nothing as well as of Being. This thinking, far from being judged by, and subjected to a procrustean measure of what is essentially inferior to it,[40] must follow its own laws.[41]

True enough, we cannot talk about The Nothing as though we were speaking of the rain outside, or a piece of chalk, or of any object whatever.[42] Since it is not-a-being, or a quality of a being, it must remain inaccessible to science.[43] But its inaccessibility to science is not a conclusive demonstration of its meaninglessness. Being itself is also inaccessible to science, since it too is not *a* being,[44] nor the quality of a being.[45] But to say that Being and The Nothing cannot be grasped by science does not say that there are no means whatever by which they might be reached.[46] While scientific and logical modes of thought are legitimate in themselves, to assert that they constitute the only valid access to reality would be a needless abridgment of human experience and a totally gratuitous impoverishment of human thought.[47] It is this that Heidegger opposes, and certainly not science or logic per se.[48]

Hence because of the circumstances at the time of his accession to the chair of philosophy at Freiburg, which found an all-triumphant science which threatened to suck all thinking into its mighty wake,

---

[37] WD, p. 99; EM, p. 92.

[38] Maurice Corvez, *La Philosophie de Heidegger* (Paris: Presses Universitaires de France, 1961), p. 84: "Nous avons pourtant un moyen de mettre en lumière ce Néant que la rigueur même de l'attitude scientifique nous dérobe. Le moyen est le phénomène de l'angoisse."

[39] EM, p. 20.

[40] EM, p. 20.

[41] HB, p. 6.

[42] WM, pp. 47-48; HB, pp. 6-7.

[43] EM, p. 19.

[44] EM, p. 19.

[45] ZS, p. 38.

[46] HB, p. 43.

[47] ZS, pp. 9, 37-38; WM, pp. 47-48.

[48] William Richardson, "Heidegger's Critique of Science," *New Scholasticism*, XLII (1968), 533-534.

the new professor wished to drive home as forcefully as possible the legitimate rights of another type of thinking. Therefore he brought the question of the Nothing to the fore, as being most fundamental to thought. In so doing he was well aware of the fact that he was forcing an issue to decision[49] — the validity of the rule of dominance of logic in metaphysics.

The question of the Nothing permeates the whole of metaphysics insofar as it compels us to face the problem of the origin of negation, i.e. ultimately it compels us to face the decision over the legitimacy of the rule of "logic" in metaphysics.[50]

Is metaphysics to be dominated by logic and its principle of contradiction which precludes any real questioning about the Nothing, or must logic itself yield to a more original manner of questioning? Is the Nothing which is indissolubly bound to the essence of Being primary and the "not" of logical propositions derivative of this, or is the "not" which is considered in negative propositions the source of all that is negative?

As Heidegger sees it, there can be no question — the Nothing which belongs to the essence of Being itself cannot be subjected to the rule of a logic which would turn it into a merely formal exercise. We can never really ask about Being or beings until we take the Nothing seriously. This is demanded by the most fundamental philosophical question:

Why is there being at all and not, rather, nothing? That is the question. Presumably it is no ordinary question. 'Why is there being at all and not, rather, nothing?' — that is manifestly *the first of all questions*.[51]

Here, and only here, when we bring the Nothing into question about Being, when we push the question of Being to its very limit, are we asking the question at the most fundamental level.[52] How is it that

---

[49] Pöggeler brings out this important point very clearly in his excellent article: "Er sucht das Seiende in der Wahrheit des Seins, im Ereignis, zu bergen. Dabei kann er nicht einfach die Logik der Metaphysik übernehmen, sondern muss eine neue Entscheidung über den Logos erzwingen." (Pöggeler, "Sein als Ereignis ...," p. 622.)

[50] "Die Frage nach dem Nichts durchgreift aber zugleich das Ganze der Metaphysik, sofern sie uns vor das Problem des Ursprungs der Verneinung zwingt, d.h. im Grunde vor die Entscheidung über die rechtmässige Herrschaft der 'Logik' in der Metaphysik." (WM, p. 40.)

[51] "Warum ist überhaupt Seiendes und nicht vielmehr Nichts? Das ist die Frage. Vermutlich ist dies keine beliebige Frage. 'Warum ist überhaupt Seiendes und nicht vielmehr Nichts?' — das ist offensichtlich *die erste aller Fragen*." (EM, p. 1.) My emphasis.

[52] EM, p. 155.

beings exist at all? How is it that they are torn away from nothingness? When we allow the Nothing to enter our consideration then the beings begin to sway and waver, and are, as it were, held in suspension, leaning back into nothingness, yet somehow held in Being. Now they are no longer taken for granted as unquestionably given data, as in the sciences, but are held out into the possibility of non-beings.[53] It is only when Nothing has been experienced, when beings are seen as ripped away from nothingness and hovering on the brink of it that we can really ask about the Being by which they exist, the primordial act of emergence from nothingness and the abiding power of gathered presence.[54]

But if Heidegger is correct, and if the consideration of the Nothing is a legitimate area of investigation for one interested in the Being-question, what would Heidegger have in mind by this Nothing? First of all the Nothing of which Heidegger speaks is not some sort of vague conceptual opposite of being in its totality. Neither is it an object of any sort,[55] or a quality of finite beings, or indeed anything that "is". Yet it is not the *nihil negativum*,[56] or *nihil absolutum* — "This Nothing to be sure is not the *nihil absolutum*."[57] That is to say, it is not pure, absolute, complete nothingness.

Just as Being when seen as the Not to being (i.e. Not-a-being) is not a Nothing in the sense of nihil negativum so also is the difference when seen as the Not between being and Being not merely a product of a distinction of the understanding (ens rationis).[58]

---

[53] On this point see for example Walter Schulz, "Über den philosophiegeschichtlichen Ort Martin Heideggers," *Philosophische Rundschau*, I (1953-54), 83.

[54] EM, pp. 21-22.

[55] HW, p. 104.

[56] As Henri Birault remarks concerning the Nothing in, "Heidegger et la pensée de la finitude," *Revue Internationale de Philosophie*, XIV (1960), 138: "... le non être n'est ici le contraire absolu de l'être, l'inexistence pure et simple, ce qui sera plus tard de *nihil negativum*. Ici encore, le non-être se présente sous les espèces de l'altérité et de lui aussi il faut bien admettre d'une certaine manière qu'il est." See also Werner Marx, *Heidegger und die Tradition* (Stuttgart: Kohlhammer, 1961), pp. 151-152.

[57] "Allerdings ist dieses Nichts nicht das nihil absolutum." (KM, p. 71.)

[58] "Aber sowenig Sein als das Nicht zum Seienden ein Nichts ist im Sinne des nihil negativum, sowenig ist die Differenz als das Nicht zwischen Seiendem und Sein nur das Gebilde einer Distinktion des Verstandes (ens rationis)." (WG, p. 5.) See also Dondeyne, "La différence ontologique ...," p. 266: "Nous nous sommes demandé ce que l'être n'est pas. Il est μὴ ὄν, non-étant, Nicht-Seiende, ce qui ... ne veut pas dire qu'il n'est rien du tout."

The Nothing does not occur by itself, apart from Being.[59] It is revealed to Dasein in the fundamental mood (*Grundstimmung*) of anxiety (*Angst*), yet not as something that is, or as a definite object.

The Nothing reveals itself in anxiety — but not as being. Nor is it given as an object.[60]

Dasein feels what-is-in-totality slipping away[61] and sees Being permeated by Nothing. It is "at one with" (*in eins mit*)[62] Being. This negativizing Nothing (*das Nichtende*)[63] which is in the very essence of Being itself is the source of the negativity which finds its expression in the negative propositions of logic.[64] If there were no negativizing element in Being prior to the negative proposition, there would be nothing for the proposition to negate. What nihilates (*das Nichten*) in Being manifests itself as the nothing-like (*das Nichthafte*). Thus the "not" (*das Nicht Seiende*) does not arise from negative statements, but rather the negative statements answer to the claim of the nihilating element in Being itself.[65]

To return now to the problem of trying to arrive at a correct interpretation of Heidegger's thought on the role of logic, and in particular to the questions which the statements contained in the inaugural address raise, we might note the following. As we saw in the last chapter it had already become clear to Heidegger by 1927 with the publication of SZ that traditional logic is possible only because man has a more primordial openness to Being. If beings were not somehow grasped in their Being in a primordial comprehension of Being, there would be no possibility of logic as a doctrine of the rules of thought. Therefore during the course of the inaugural lecture Heidegger attempts to show that the "not" of the assertion is of a derivative sort, having its source in the Nothing,[66] which is bound up with Being.[67] In the foundational thought that was attempted in SZ the positive assertion which was examined in the light of the Being-question was seen to require a more ultimate ground in the pre-ontological comprehension

---

[59] WM, p. 35.

[60] "Das Nichts enthüllt sich in der Angst — aber nicht als Seiendes. Es wird ebensowenig als Gegenstand gegeben." (WM, p. 33.)

[61] WM, p. 32.

[62] WM, p. 33.

[63] HB, p. 44.

[64] HB, pp. 43-44.

[65] HB, pp. 43-44.

[66] WM, p. 36.

[67] WM, pp. 35, 39.

of Being. In WM we have moved a step farther — the negative proposition cannot be interpreted in the most ultimate way unless it is also seen within this same perspective of Being, but whereas the positive proposition derives from a primordial grasp of Being, the negative proposition derives from the Nothing. In terms of the positive assertion, Dasein is open to Being through comprehension, disposition and λόγος. As to the negative proposition, Dasein is also open to the Nothing through one of its fundamental moods, Angst and in this mood the Nothing is revealed,[68] which, in its turn, is the ultimate ground of all negativity. In SZ, the ultimate grounding of the positive proposition had been disclosed. In WM, the ultimate grounding of the negative proposition has now also been revealed.

What Heidegger is saying, then, in the statement of WM is not that all logic is to be discarded as valueless, but rather he is attempting to show that it is not the *only* approach to thought. There is, therefore, a very definite reason for placing the word "logic" in quotes — it is to be taken in a special sense. The "logic" which is placed in quotes is the unquestioned dominance of "logic", "logic" as the *only* approach to thought, the "logical" thinking that has dominated Western metaphysics. If this is clear, then it is also clear that the legitimate areas of logic are in no way impugned, or included in this "attack". Heidegger does not by any means wish to suggest that all logic is worthless, an impediment to thought, a 2,000 year long mistake, or anything of the sort.[69] To interpret him in this way would be nonsense. What is called into question in this so-called "attack" on logic in WM is the previously unquestioned assumption that it is the only mode of philosophic thought, the court of last appeal in philosophy. For a thought which thinks on Being as truth, that is, simultaneous revelation *and concealment*, for a thought which thinks on Being and the Nothing, another approach is required. Therefore if we understand Heidegger in an adequate way we see that the legitimate rights of logic are in no way called into question. Logic, as such, is not rejected or to be discarded. It is only the unquestioned assumption that the "logical" way of thought which has characterized Western metaphysics is the *only* way of thought that is called into question. The point that Heidegger

---

[68] WM, pp. 32-33.

[69] This point is again clarified in the lecture course of 1935 which was published in 1953 as EM: "Deshalb muss 'die Logik' in Anführungszeichen gesetzt werden. Dies geschieht nicht deshalb, weil wir 'das Logische' (im Sinne des recht Gedachten) verleugnen wollen." (EM, p. 92.)

is attempting to make is that it is *one* way of thought, legitimate, worth-while, and valuable, but it is not the *only* way. Therefore in the statements of the inaugural address the legitimate areas of logical investigation are in no way impugned.[70]

From this it becomes clear that for Heidegger the negative proposition is derivative in character. If the principle of contradiction precludes a primordial questioning about the Nothing it is obviously not the most basic principle of metaphysics, given the centrality of the question of the Nothing to the Being-question. Further, if the principle of contradiction is itself the cornerstone of logic, then the role of logic in metaphysics will be limited: it is not the most fundamental science within metaphysics.

... the principle of contradiction is not a basic principle of metaphysics ... Logic cannot be the fundamental science for metaphysics.[71]

[70] Pöggeler in his analysis of this text from WM, pp. 36-37 suggests the following interpretation in the light of Heidegger's basic concern — thinking through to Being as truth: "Auch in dem neuen Ansatz geht Heidegger aus von der Grunderfahrung, dass die traditionelle, die 'logische' Weise des Denkens für die heute nötige Frage nach dem Sein nicht zureicht: wird dem Sein das Nichts zugedacht, macht sich das Denken bereit, das Sein in seiner Wahrheit als das unverfügbare Ereignis zu erfahren, dann entscheidet sich 'das Schicksal der Herrschaft der 'Logik' innerhalb der Philosophie': 'Die Idee der "Logik" selbst löst sich auf im Wirbel eines ursprünglicheren Fragens.' Das hier genannte Fragen ist ursprünglicher als das metaphysische Fragen nach dem Sein, weil es die vergessene Wahrheit des Seins zum Problem macht. Die Idee der 'Logik', die sich in diesem Fragen auflöst, ist die Selbstverständlichkeit der Herrschaft, ja der Alleinherrschaft des 'logischen' Denkens in der Philosophie. Das 'ursprünglichere' Fragen wendet sich polemisch dagegen, dass die überlieferte Logik die Möglichkeiten des Denkens soll ausschöpfen können, *aber es tastet das begrenzte sachliche Recht der Logik nicht an.*" (*Der Denkweg* ..., p. 273.) My emphasis.

[71] "... ist der Satz vom Widerspruch kein Grundsatz der Metaphysik ... Die Logik kann nicht die Grundwissenschaft der Metaphysik sein." (DF, p. 137.)

CHAPTER IV

LOGIC VERSUS AUTHENTIC THOUGHT

Let us summarize briefly the salient points of the argument thus far presented and from them project a glance toward what will be developed in the pages which lie ahead. First, Heidegger's basic concern from the beginning of his way has been with the meaning of Being, or Being as truth. Second, the very core of his thought lies in his understanding of truth, ἀλήθεια, as simultaneous revelation and self-concealment. Third, the history of Western metaphysics has been characterized by its singular forgetfulness of the difference between Being and beings, or Being in its revelatory power as truth. The portion of Heidegger's way that we are now about to traverse, thinking, is the Archimedean point of the whole logic problematic, and Heidegger could not be clearer on this point:

We must recognize in the apparently casual separation of *Being and thought* that fundamental position of the spirit of the West *against which our real attack is directed.*[1]

Thinking, since Plato, has been treated under the title of logic[2] — the formation of ideas, the rules which govern their union with one another in the proposition, and the linking of these propositions in the syllogistic process. Logic of this sort, in Heidegger's view, is not incorrect, but it is inadequate,[3] i.e. it does not take in the full amplitude of the richness of man's union with Being which issues in authentic thought. What kind of thinking is adequate for the grasp of Being in its unique difference, Being in its truth?[4] A thinking which thinks on the truth

---

[1] "Wir müssen in der scheinbar gleichgültigen Scheidung *Sein und Denken* jene Grundstellung des Geistes des Abendlandes erkennen, *der unser eigentlicher Angriff gilt.*" (EM, p. 89.) My emphasis.

[2] WD, p. 105. Cf. also ED, 108, 119-120, 126-127; EM, pp. 91-93; KTS, p. 35; DF, p. 113.

[3] WD, p. 126; EM, p. 92; WM, p. 47.

[4] EM, p. 92.

of Being can no longer content itself with the notion of thought which has prevailed in the Western metaphysical tradition.[5] The question which we must now attempt to answer is, what does Heidegger understand by thinking, not as the word is so glibly used, or in his view abused, today, but a thinking which is appropriate to that which gives itself to thought? The answer which is given to this question will be decisive for an understanding of his position on logic, since his critique of logic must be situated within what is for him the larger question, the problem of thought — what type of thinking is an adequate response to Being as truth? As Heidegger sees it, it will not be the type of thought which has characterized traditional metaphysics, that is, a thought subjected to the rigid rules of Aristotelian logic. Thought, at least in the plenary Heideggerian sense, will be ruled rather by the command (*Geheiss*) of Being.

Therefore, in order to determine the nature of thought, which is for Heidegger the key issue for the logic problematic, we must first examine the foundation of thought, Being as truth. In other words in order to determine *what* thought is ("*Was* heisst Denken") we must first determine what *evokes* thought ("Was *heisst* Denken"), i.e. Being.[6] Since thought is a response to Being, in order to know what type of thought will be an adequate response to Being, we must first see what Heidegger understands by Being. Accordingly, we shall take under consideration in this chapter the key Heideggerian notions of Being as truth, φύσις-ἀλήθεια, and thinking which is a response to the call (*Geheiss*) of Being, νοεῖν. We shall attempt to show that thought is ruled by the command (*Geheiss*) of Being because of the intimate union of φύσις-ἀλήθεια, λόγος, νοεῖν, and ἐὸν ἔμμεναι with each other. The importance of these steps to the logic problematic is clear: what is being asserted is that the command of Being, rather than logic and the assertion, is the first rule of thought that thinks on Being as truth. First of all we shall attempt to explicate Heidegger's notion of truth, which, as he sees it, first revealed itself to the Greeks as φύσις-ἀλήθεια. We shall also see why it should happen that truth should be transformed from ἀλήθεια into ἰδέα, and as a consequence of this changed nature of truth that it should also change its locus to the assertion. Truth, ἀλήθεια, becomes correspondence of thought and thing. This finds its expression in the well-known medieval dictum, "veritas est adaequatio

---

[5] As Heidegger remarks in WM, p. 9: "Ein Denken, das an die Wahrheit des Seins denkt, begnügt sich zwar nicht mehr mit der Metaphysik ..."

[6] WD, p. 83.

intellectus et rei." We shall leave this point, the origin and development of logic undeveloped for the moment, since we shall take it up in detail in the next chapter.

Being first disclosed itself to the early Greeks, according to Heidegger, as φύσις.[7] In examining the etymological root of this word he finds that it is related to the verb φύω,[8] which means to emerge, to be powerful, of itself to come to a stand[9] and to remain.[10] It is also related to the radical φα- (φαινεσθαι), to flare up, to show itself to appear.[11] As the early Greeks experienced Being it had both the aspect of overpowering, emerging from concealment[12] by a lighting process, and also coming to a stand and appearing.[13] The usual translation, which is not only a translation but also an interpretation according to Heidegger, has customarily rendered these words as "nature" or "to grow."[14] What φύσις really denotes, however, is a self-blossoming emergence,[15] an unfolding which reveals itself in the act of unfolding and perseveres in it.[16] Instances of it are as multiple as are beings — in the unfolding of a rose through some mysterious intrinsic power, in the emergence from the mother's womb of a man or animal.[17] But φύσις itself which is the primordial power by which beings appear and come into presence[18] is not to be identified with any one, or with the totality of beings, a tendency to which Dasein all too readily succumbs since it is so intimately tied to the individual beings which have emerged from concealment and are present to it.

Now it can be easily seen that the beings which are present, for example the earth, the sea, the mountains, plants and animals, are always open to us. Therefore beings are familiar and directly accessible to us. That by which each of these beings which are emerging into presence emerge into presence and come forth, each after its own fashion is never face-to-face with us as the beings

---

[7] As Heidegger notes in SG, p. 154: "Sein schickt sich dem frühen griechischen Denken unter anderem als φύσις."

[8] EM, p. 11.

[9] EM, p. 12.

[10] EM, p. 139.

[11] EM, pp. 54, 76-77.

[12] EM, p. 145.

[13] EM, p. 83.

[14] Vom Wesen und Begriff der Φύσις. Aristoteles Physik B, 1, contained in Wegmarken (Frankfurt a. M.: Klostermann, 1967), pp. 309, 329. Hereafter P. Cf. also EM, pp. 10-11.

[15] DF, p. 64.

[16] EM, p. 147. Cf. also P, in Wegmarken, p. 324.

[17] EM, p. 11.

[18] EM, p. 106.

which are here and there present. Being is by no means so directly familiar and manifest to us as being.[19]

It is not one process among the many phenomena which may be observed in nature. It is Being itself opening up and jutting out beyond itself while retaining its immanent power of presenting itself. "Being is the self-concealing revelation — φύσις in the original sense."[20]

This emerging (Aufgehen) and in-itself-standing-out-from-itself may not be taken as a process among others which we observe in being. Φύσις is Being itself in virtue of which alone being becomes and remains observable.[21]

Thus the very essence of Being is φύσις — "Being essences itself as φύσις."[22] It is the intrinsic power by which it emerges from concealment,[23] stands in the light, or blazes forth[24] in revelation, and appears.[25] And further it is that power by which beings come forth into presence and endure.[26] What is of importance in terms of the logic problematic is that this presencing of Being (Anwesen) is overpowering, it bursts upon Dasein, Dasein is shattered against it. Obviously, it is not something which is conceptual.[27] Further Being as presence is presence (pre-sense).[28] To put it another way Dasein is so structured that it is open to Being,[29] which is, as it were, pre-sent to it.[30] This is simply the obverse side of what we have already seen in re Dasein's pre-conceptual comprehension of Being, but looked at now from Being's standpoint. This is not,

---

[19] "Nun zeigt sich überall leicht, dass uns das jeweilig Seiende, z.B. die Erde, das Meer, die Gebirge, die Gewächse und die Tiere, jederzeit offenkundig gegenüberliegt. Darum ist es uns vertraut und unmittelbar zugänglich. Dagegen liegt das, wohindurch all dieses von-sich-her-Anwesende auf seine Weise anwest und aufgeht, uns niemals gegenüber wie das hier und dort jeweils Anwesende. Das Sein ist uns keineswegs so unmittelbar vertraut und offenkundig wie das jeweilig Seiende. (SG, p. 111.)

[20] "Sein ist das sich verbergende Entbergen — φύσις im anfänglichen Sinne." (P, in Wegmarken, p. 371.)

[21] "Dieses Aufgehen und In-sich-aus-sich-Hinausstehen darf nicht als ein Vorgang genommen werden, den wir unter anderen am Seienden beobachten. Die φύσις ist das Sein selbst, kraft dessen das Seiende erst beobachtbar wird und bleibt." (EM, p. 11.)

[22] "Sein west als φύσις." (EM, p. 77.)

[23] EM, p. 141. Cf. also SG, p. 114; P, in Wegmarken, pp. 370-371.

[24] "... dieser Aufblitz des Seins ..." (VA, p. 227.) My emphasis.

[25] EM, p. 77. Cf. also EM, p. 83.

[26] EM, p. 77.

[27] EM, p. 47.

[28] As Seidel suggests in, Heidegger and Presocratics ..., p. 47, note.

[29] HW, p. 83.

[30] EM, p. 134.

to be sure, to be understood as a naive ontologism.[31] Heidegger's purpose here it must be remembered is to overcome the severing of Being from thought,[32] as we have already seen.

Since in coming to presence, in appearing, Being emerges from concealment[33] it was also named by the Greeks ἀλήθεια, truth.[34] This Greek word is composed of two elements, the first, the alpha privative,[35] and the root, λήθη, meaning veil. Being, then, in emerging from concealment[36] dis-closes itself, unveils itself.[37] It is a process of lighting in which it is wrested from concealment, or re-vealed. Here it might be well to note that some classical scholars, most notably Friedländer,[38] have very serious reservations about the legitimacy of Heidegger's assertion that for the Greeks truth, ἀλήθεια,[39] was originally re-velation. We shall

[31] As John Wild considers it in, "An English Version of Martin Heidegger's *Being and Time*," *Review of Metaphysics*, XVI (1962), 311. In a similar vein see Fritz Heinemann, *Existenzphilosophie — lebendig oder tot?* (Stuttgart: Kohlhammer, 1963), p. 104; Huch, *Philosophiegeschichtliche Voraussetzungen* ..., pp. 8, 18-20; Ernst Konrad Specht, *Sprache und Sein: Untersuchungen zur sprachanalytischen Grundlegung der Ontologie* (Berlin: De Gruyter, 1967), p. 41.

[32] EM, p. 106.

[33] EM, p. 87.

[34] EM, pp. 47, 77, 78, 144-145; KM, pp. 115, 206.

[35] PL, p. 32; SZ, p. 222.

[36] WW, p. 19.

[37] KM, p. 115.

[38] Paul Friedländer, *Plato*, tr. Hans Meyerhoff (New York: Pantheon, 1958), I, 221-229. E. Heitsch, on the other hand, shows in two studies that the word ἀλήθεια did have the meaning of revelation for the early Greeks. See his studies, "Wahrheit als Erinnerung," *Hermes*, XCI (1963), 36-53; "Die nicht-philosophische Aletheia," *Hermes*, XC (1962), 24-33. H. Boeder raises the further question that even if it be granted that ἀλήθεια meant revelation, as he thinks it did, what did revelation mean to the early Greeks? On this point see his article, "Der frühgriechische Wortgebrauch von Logos und Aletheia," *Archiv für Begriffsgeschichte*, IV (1959), 82-112. For other criticisms of Heidegger's use of etymology and language, cf. for example Rudolf Boehm, "Pensée et technique," *Revue Internationale de Philosophie*, XIV (1960), 194-220: Frederick Van de Pitte, "The role of Hölderlin in the Philosophy of Heidegger," *The Personalist*, XLII (1962), 168-179; Clarence Richey, "On the Intentional Ambiguity of Heidegger's Metaphysics," *Journal of Philosophy*, LV (1958), 1144-1148; Marjorie Glicksman, "A Note on the Philosophy of Heidegger," *Journal of Philosophy*, XXXV (1938), 93-104; Karsten Harries, "Heidegger and Hölderlin; The Limits of Language," *Personalist*, XLIV (1963), 5-23; Walter Kaufman, *From Shakespeare to Existentialism* (New York: Doubleday 1960), p. 339; Arthur Adkins, "Heidegger and Language," *Philosophy*, XXXVII (1962), 229-237. See also Ernst Tugendhat, "*Der Wahrheitsbegriff bei Husserl und Heidegger*", ... pp. 260-261.

[39] PL, pp. 26-33, 36, 40-52; HW, pp. 39-40, 48, 142, 310-311, 320-326, 341; VA, pp. 19, 28, 53, 182, 220, 247, 248, 250-255, 257-282; WD, p. 126; SZ, pp. 33-35; WW, pp. 15-16, 19, 26.

not enter into a prolonged examination of the merits of Friedländer's position. Suffice it to say that Heidegger has gone out of his way on innumerable occasions to point out that he is not doing etymological studies as a classical philologist does them.[40] He has indicated in the clearest terms possible that he is not interested in etymologies for their own sake.[41] In terms of the philosophic task which he proposes for himself this type of endeavor would be simply an uncreative repetition of the past.[42] Rather, he is interested in recovering what was concealed in the very revelation of Being that was caught up in language.[43] This concealment which occurs in language is attributable principally to two causes. The first is the self-concealing character of the revelation of Being itself.[44] Its revelation always contains an undisclosed fullness — "The origin on the contrary always contains the unopened fullness ..."[45] And thus Heidegger is not interested in simply going back to the pre-socratics and determining with historical exactitude what various key words meant, since even at the beginning when Being first blazed forth so brightly[46] there was at the same time a forgetfulness of Being. The fullness of the revelation could not be totally comprehended by Dasein because of the concealing character of the revelation itself.

The breakdown in unconcealment, as we call that happening in a summary fashion, does not, to be sure, spring from a pure lack, an inability to bear that which was confided with this essence to the custody of historical man. The ground of the breakdown lies first of all in the greatness of the origin and in the essence of the origin itself.[47]

[40] See for example EM, p. 124, 134; WD, pp. 83-84, 90.

[41] HW, pp. 301-303; WD, pp. 83, 122.

[42] Thus Heidegger, in an interview in the French magazine *L'Express* answered the question: "Pensez-vous qu'il faille retourner aux sources de la pensée grecque?" Heidegger: "Retourner? Une renaissance moderne de l'antiquité? Ce serait absurde, et d'ailleurs impossible. La pensée grecque ne peut être qu'un point de départ." (*Express*, N, 954, 20-26, Oct. 1969, p. 80). Cf. also HW, pp. 39-40.

[43] ID, pp. 44-45. Our treatment here will not attempt to do justice to such complex notions as the "Wiederholung," or its relation to the past, present and future of time, or Heidegger's dialogue with the great thinkers of the past. Interesting and important as these topics are, they would, unfortunately, take us much too far afield.

[44] EM, p. 87.

[45] "Der Anfang dagegen enthält immer die unerschlossene Fülle ..." (HW, p. 63.)

[46] EM, pp. 12, 119.

[47] "Der Einsturz der Unverborgenheit, wie wir jenes Geschehnis kurz nennen, entspringt allerdings nicht einem blossen Mangel, einem nicht mehr Tragen-können dessen was mit diesem Wesen dem geschichtlichen Menschen zur Bewahrung aufgegeben war. Der Grund des Einsturzes liegt zuerst in der Grösse des Anfangs und im Wesen des Anfangs selbst." (EM, p. 145.) Cf. also EM, p. 111; WD, p. 42.

Hence a mere repetitive imitation of the past would be essentially sterile.[48]

The second cause of concealment which occurs in language derives from the very nature of language as something which is uttered. What is first named in the word[49] out of an intimate union of thought and Being is said over and over again,[50] and is progressively emptied of meaningfulness.[51] The word is heard and understood but the experience of Being which it names is not. The word is much like a coin which is passed from hand to hand until the image which it bore originally is gradually effaced and it is no longer recognizable.

This process of concealment of the original Being-experience is especially promoted by the passage of philosophic words from one language to another.

With this Latin translation, however, the primordial concentration of the Greek word φύσις is already pushed aside, the authentic philosophic naming power (*Nennkraft*) of the Greek word destroyed. This is true not only of the Latin translation of *this* word, but of all other translations of Greek philosophic language into the Roman. The procedure of this translation of the Greek into Roman is not harmless and a matter of indifference, but the first stage of the process of blocking and alienation from the original essence (*Wesen*) of Greek philosophy.[52]

Being, experienced by the Greeks as φύσις, ἀλήθεια, λόγος, is translated into latin as *natura, veritas, ratio*. The word is taken over but the experience of Being which gave rise to the word is not had at all.

The names which are the issue of naming are not just arbitrary names (*Benennungen*). In these names something speaks which can no longer be shown — *the fundamental Greek experience of the Being of being.*[53]

But the basis of language is the experience of what is expressed in the word. Hence we have in the West a philosophic tradition which is

---

[48] EM, p. 96; WD, p. 110.

[49] WD, p. 85.

[50] EM, p. 141.

[51] SZ, pp. 167-170; EM, pp. 38, 39, 132; WD, p. 83.

[52] "Mit dieser lateinischen Übersetzung wird aber schon der ursprüngliche Gehalt des griechischen Wortes φύσις abgedrängt, die eigentliche philosophische Nennkraft des griechischen Wortes zerstört. Das gilt nicht nur von der lateinischen Übersetzung *dieses* Wortes, sondern von allen anderen Übersetzungen der griechischen Philosophensprache ins Römische. Der Vorgang dieser Übersetzung des Griechischen ins Römische ist nichts Beliebiges und Harmloses, sondern der erste Abschnitt des Verlaufs der Abriegelung und Entfremdung des ursprünglichen Wesens der griechischen Philosophie." (EM, pp. 10-11.)

[53] "Diese Benennungen sind keine beliebigen Namen. In ihnen spricht, was hier nicht mehr zu zeigen ist, *die griechische Grunderfahrung des Seins des Seienden* überhaupt." (HW, p. 12.) My emphasis.

essentially without foundation since it is founded upon a translation of the Greek language without the primordial experience of Being which was the fecundating source of language. The translation, "*Übersetzung*," is indeed a *trans*-lation, *Über*-setzung, a process in which the basis of the words in question is completely passed over.[54]

The translation of the Greek names into the Latin language is, to be sure, by no means the harmless process for which it is held to be even today. Rather, concealing itself behind apparently literal, and therefore faithful translation (Übersetzung) is a *trans*-lating (*Über*setzen) of the Greek experience into another form of thought. Roman thought takes over the Greek words without a corresponding experience which is as primordial as the Greek of that which is spoken, without the Greek words. The foundationlessness of Western thought begins (*beginnt*) with this translation.[55]

Heidegger, then, is not interested in going back to word roots to determine with the exactness of the philologist the meaning of a word. The work of the philosopher, at least as he conceives of the task of philosophy, starts where the work of philology stops,[56] or more precisely the one is on the level of what Heidegger calls *Historie*,[57] determination of what the past was as past (*Vergangenheit*), while the other is not interested in the past as past, but sees it as somehow living still (*Gewesenheit*) and influencing the present and future.[58] But if the future is to be shaped according to its authentic possibilities the past cannot be simply taken over in an imitative, essentially uncreative repetition. Instead it must be "destroyed",[59] which is not to be understood as a sophomoric attempt to refute positions of the past. It has rather the positive sense of attempting to break through structures

---

[54] P, in *Wegmarken*, p. 315.

[55] "Freilich ist diese Übersetzung der griechischen Namen in die lateinische Sprache keineswegs der harmlose Vorgang für den er noch heutigentags gehalten wird. Vielmehr verbirgt sich hinter der anscheinend wörtlichen und somit bewahrenden Übersetzung ein *Über*setzen griechischer Erfahrung in eine andere Denkungsart. Das römische Denken übernimmt die griechischen Wörter ohne die entsprechende gleichursprüngliche Erfahrung dessen, was sie sagen, ohne das griechische Wort. Die Bodenlosigkeit des abendländischen Denkens beginnt mit diesem Übersetzen." (HW, p. 13.)

[56] HW, p. 343; WD, p. 91.

[57] HW, p. 76. Cf. also HW, pp. 80, 302; VA, pp. 63-64; N, II, pp. 483, 489; HB, pp. 23-24.

[58] PL, p. 50.

[59] On the sense of "destruction" see especially SZ, No. 6, "Die Aufgabe einer Destruktion der Geschichte der Ontologie", pp. 19-27. Also EM, pp. 134, 135; HB, p. 23; HW, pp. 302, 343; ID, pp. 44, 45, 48; KM, pp. 182, 183, 185; PL, p. 25; WD, pp. 89, 91, 110; WP, pp. 15, 20, 27. 31, 33-34, 44.

which have become hardened and rigid with the passage of time in order to reclaim Being's revelation. To "repeat" the original commencement (*Anfang*), then, does not mean repetition in the sense of a slavish aping of the past.[60] The repetition of the origin (*Anfang*) must be a new and original experience of the origin (*Anfang*) as origin (*Anfang*) and thus an original experience of Being in its own right.[61]

Thus objections to Heidegger's use of etymologies are in most instances beside the point.[62] His study of a word's etymology or his entering into a dialogue with a great thinker of the past is not simply to determine with precision what a word meant at a given period in history, or what a great thinker said. It is precisely to get at what was *not* said, what was *not* thought, and moreover *could not* be. His purpose, then, in going to the past will be in function of his understanding of truth as self-concealing revelation. Because of the undisclosed fullness of Being's revelation as it was expressed in the original naming and in the authentic thought of the great philosophers of the past it is worthy of being reexamined. Because, however, it was a concealing revelation, merely to go back to what was said or thought, rather than to what was left unsaid and unthought, would simply be a repetition of the initial forgetfulness.

To repeat (*wiederholen*) the origin (*Anfang*)[63] means to break through the hardened, and now hollow, shells of words to get at what was first revealed.[64] But since the revelation at the great beginning was itself shot through with concealment, there can be no question of simply digging back into the past to regain a buried treasure. The origin (*Anfang*) itself must be begun (*anfängt*) in a new way and more radically than before. To repeat (*wieder-holen*), or better, to retrieve,[65] means:

An original commencing however is not retrieved by turning back to the past as past and now known which is simply to be imitated. To retrieve the origin (*Anfang*) is to originate it again (*wiederangefangen*) more originally, and indeed

[60] SZ, p. 41; KM, p. 183.

[61] EM, pp. 145-146.

[62] As Richardson points out: "Es hätte wenig Sinn, Heidegger mit den Massstaben 'wissenschaftlicher' Philologie oder Historie kritisieren zu wollen. Gerade weil er seine Aufgabe selbst als ein Sagen dessen charakterisiert, was seine Gesprächspartner nicht gesagt haben, ist sein Gespräch mit anderen immer eine Wiederholung und deshalb eine Auslegung seiner eigen Erfahrung." ("Heideggers Weg ...," p. 396.)

[63] KM, p. 185.

[64] EM, p. 11.

[65] The translation suggested by Richardson, *Through Phenomenology ...*, p. 89.

with all the strangeness, darkness, and insecurity that attend a true originating (*Anfang*).[66]

Let us return now to our consideration of φύσις-ἀλήθεια. In seeing truth as simultaneous[67] revelation and concealment,[68] Heidegger can remark, "The essence of truth is untruth."[69] What are we to make of such a statement? From what we have already seen its meaning should be clear. Truth is untruth in the sense that it is not only revelation, but at the same time, necessarily, self-concealment and withdrawal. The untruth spoken of is not to be understood as the *logical* opposite of truth, falsity.

The statement: the essence of truth is untruth, does not mean to say that truth is fundamentally falsity.[70]

It is the veil which shrouds and conceals Being even in its revelation. This is as it must be, since if Being were pure uncoveredness, pure openness, where would be the *re*-velation, the drawing back of the veil?

... Self-concealment belongs to Being. This in no way means to say that Being is nothing other than self-concealment, but rather: Being indeed essences itself as φύσις, as self-revelation, of what is manifest in itself, but that self-concealment belongs to it. If the concealment were lacking, how then would revealing happen?[71]

If, on the other hand, it were concealment pure and simple, it would also not be itself and would not be the process by which beings are lighted up and made to appear.[72] Hence, to drive home as forcefully as possible both aspects of truth, that is, both self-concealment and self-revelation, Heidegger chooses the striking phrase, "the essence of truth is untruth."

---

[66] "Ein Anfang wird aber nicht wiederholt, indem man sich auf ihn als ein Vormaliges und nunmehr Bekanntes und lediglich Nachzumachendes zurückschreibt, sondern indem der Anfang *ursprünglicher* wiederangefangen wird und zwar mit all dem Befremdlichen, Dunklen, Ungesicherten, das ein wahrhafter Anfang bei sich führt." (EM, p. 29.)

[67] WW, p. 23.

[68] WD, p. 8. Cf. also WW, pp. 17, 19.

[69] "Das Wesen der Wahrheit ist die Un-wahrheit." (HW, p. 43.) Cf. also WW, p. 19.

[70] "Der Satz: das Wesen der Wahrheit ist die Un-Wahrheit, soll dagegen nicht sagen, die Wahrheit sei im Grund Falschheit." (HW, p. 49.) See also Else Buddeberg, *Heidegger und die Dichtung: Hölderlin, Rilke* (Stuttgart: Metzlesche, 1953), p. 16.

[71] "... zum Sein gehört ein Sichverbergen. Damit sagt er keineswegs, Sein sei nichts anderes als Sichverbergen, sondern: Sein west zwar als φύσις, als Sichentbergen, von sich des Offenkundiges aber dazu gehört Sichverbergen. Fiele die Verbergung aus und weg, wie sollte dann noch Entbergung geschehen?" (SG, pp. 113-114.)

[72] P, in *Wegmarken*, pp. 370-371.

Truth, then, is a primordial struggle (*Urstreit*)[73] between opposites, light and darkness, revelation and concealment.[74] It is not to be identified with the one or the other. In order to indicate Being's penchant for concealment[75] Heidegger frequently cites a maxim of Heraclitus, φύσις κρύπτεσθαι φιλεῖ,[76] Being is fond of hiding itself.[77] Being, as φύσις, emerges from concealment,[78] but in its very self-manifestation, ἀλήθεια, concealment already prevails. This is necessarily so, since φιλεῖ means to love, which means to be as one, to belong together (*zusammengehören*). Both self-revelation and self-concealment are so intimately and inextricably bound to Being that they can never be separated from it.

Already before Plato and Aristotle, Heraclitus, one of the early Greek thinkers, had said φύσις κρυπτεσθαι φιλεῖ (Frg. 123): Being loves self-concealment. Yet what does φιλεῖ, to love, mean, if thought according to the Greek mind? It means to belong together in one. Heraclitus wishes to say: self-concealment belongs to Being.[79]

From these considerations we are now in a position to see how Being as truth, ἀλήθεια, could be transformed into ἰδέα, and ultimately to what is expressed by the assertion. First Being intrinsically tends to conceal itself. It blazed forth and was experienced by the Greeks as φύσις, overpowering emergence into presence, and as ἀλήθεια, revelation wrested from concealment,[80] and primordial struggle of lighting and occultation. But this manifestation of Being was quickly concealed. We shall not, at the moment, pursue this line of inquiry, that is, the transformation of truth, ἀλήθεια, into ἰδέα and its relation to the development of logic, since this will be the burden of the next chapter.

We have seen now, if only in the barest outline, how Heidegger conceives of Being as φύσις-ἀλήθεια. It is this Being which e-vokes (*heisst*) thought. The question which now confronts us is this — what is the nature of thought which will be an adequate response to the

[73] HW, pp. 43, 49.

[74] This point is brought out for example by John Anderson in his essay, "Truth, Process, and Creature," *Heidegger and the Quest for Truth* ..., pp. 58-60.

[75] SZ, p. 311; WW, pp. 21-23.

[76] EM, p. 87.

[77] P, in *Wegmarken*, p. 370.

[78] P, in *Wegmarken*, pp. 370-371.

[79] "Schon vor Platon und Aristoteles hat einer der frühen griechischen Denker, Heraklit, gesagt: φύσις κρυπτεσθαι φιλεῖ (Frg. 123): Sein liebt (ein) Sichverbergen. Doch was heisst, griechisch gedacht, φιλεῖ, lieben? Es heisst: zusammengehören im Selben. Heraklit will sagen: Zum Sein gehört ein Sichverbergen." (SG, p. 113.)

[80] PL, p. 32.

invitation of Being? In reflecting on the nature of thinking in our scientific age, with all of its intense cerebral activity, with its drive for exactness and rigor in thought, in the last series of university lectures at Freiburg (1951-52) before his formal retirement from the university, Heidegger was led to remark, "the most thought-provoking thing about this thought-provoking age of ours is that we are still not thinking."[81] But what can be the meaning of this enigmatic statement? Is it not blatantly contradicted by the most obvious facts of our daily existence? Has there ever been an age before us which has given such a high priority to thought? After all, billions of dollars and countless hours are given over to its cultivation in our schools. We have our "think-tanks" which harness the mental energies of our greatest minds. We have research teams which have accomplished, through Herculean efforts of cerebration, incredible feats of thinking in medicine, in space travel, in cybernetics, in communications, and indeed in every field of knowledge. Given all of this frenzied mental activity, what can be the meaning of this lapidary aphorism by which the recluse of Todtnauberg has characterized our scientific age as thought-less?[82] What, as Heidegger understands it, is thinking?

Thinking, so Heidegger contends, as it is understood in our contemporary milieu, is identified with what is done in the sciences,[83] whose foundation is ultimately logico-mathematical." ... The basic feature of our modern thought and knowledge, in the authentic sense, is mathe-

---

[81] "Das Bedenklichste in unserer bedenklichen Zeit ist, dass wir noch nicht denken." (WD, p. 3.)

[82] On the meaning, purpose and scope of Heidegger's critique of science see for example, Richardson, "Heidegger's Critique of Science ...", pp. 511-536. Karlfried Gründer, "M. Heideggers Wissenschaftskritik in ihren geschichtlichen Zusammenhängen," *Archiv für Philosophie*, XI (1962), 312-335, in evaluating Heidegger's critique of science sees it as part of the romantic tradition (pp. 321-322). Starting from the attempt to ground metaphysics anew, an opposition is created between thought (as thinkers think) and scientific thought. This produces a pseudo-philosophy which is, in the final analysis, a surrogate religion form, a mythologizing of Being (p. 330). He remarks on p. 332: "Im Werke Martin Heideggers verbindet sich anfangs der wissenschaftskritische Impuls mit dem Versuch einer Neubegründung. In den späteren Schriften jedoch hat sich die Verfallstheorie der Geschichte so durchgesetzt, dass Wissenschaft und Denken in einer betonten Entgegensetzung stehen, geschieden durch eine unüberbrückbare Kluft. Instanz für Heideggers Wissenschaftskritik ist sein Sonderbegriff des Denkens, der nach Ursprung und Intention *nicht genuin philosophisch* ist, sondern den Charakter eines *religiösen Surrogates romantischer Herkunft* hat." My emphasis.

[83] On this point see for example Walter Otto, "Die Zeit und das Sein," *Anteile: Martin Heidegger zum 60. Geburtstag* (Frankfurt: Klostermann, 1950), p. 7.

matical."[84] Science has become the very paradigm of thinking.[85] What is thinking today? Thinking is what the scientists do. The rules which govern its operation and insure its rigor are given by logic[86] and mathematics.[87] But the question must be asked, is this the *only* way of thinking,[88] and further, is the logico-mathematico-scientific method of thought the ultimate ground and measure of thought, or do logic, mathematics and science themselves stand in need of a foundation?

The most thought-provoking thing about this thought-provoking are in which we live is that we are still, in spite of all of the frenetic mental activity expended by the sciences, not thinking. Science in fact does not "think" at all, at least as Heidegger understands the word, as thinkers do — "Science does not think in the sense of the thinking of the thinkers."[89] It was born at the precise moment in history when thought ceased — "... science appears, thought disappears."[90] Science, and logic as the explication of the formal structure and rules of thought, came into existence when Being, ἐὸν ἔμμεναι, was transformed from φύσις-ἀλήθεια into ἰδέα.[91] Thinking which had been experienced as νοεῖν which was united to Being is transformed into "philosophy," and "philosophy" becomes a science.

Thought becomes 'philosophy', philosophy becomes ἐπιστήμη (science) and science itself becomes a thing for schools and the school curriculum.[92]

By the severing of truth and thinking from Being, thought is torn away from its life-giving element.[93] Just as a branch can only live when it is in vital organic unity with the vine, so thought can only flourish according to its true nature when vitally united to Being. Cut from its source, it is fore-doomed to wither and eventually die.[94]

---

[84] DF, p. 59. Cf. also HW, pp. 71-76.

[85] VA, pp. 46-47; HB, p. 6; ZS, pp. 37-38.

[86] WD, p. 10. Cf. also WD, pp. 102, 119-120; EM, pp. 91-92; DF, p. 113.

[87] EM, p. 147-148.

[88] WM, p. 47; WD, p. 10.

[89] "Die Wissenschaft denkt nicht im Sinne des Denkens der Denker." (WD, p. 154.) Cf. also WD, p. 4.

[90] "... entsteht die Wissenschaft, vergeht das Denken." (HB, p. 39.)

[91] EM, pp. 92-93.

[92] "... das Denken zur 'Philosophie' die Philosophie aber zur ἐπιστήμη (Wissenschaft) und die Wissenschaft selbst zu einer Sache der Schule und des Schulbetriebs werden lässt." (HB, p. 39.) Cf. also EM, pp. 91-92.

[93] WM, p. 8.

[94] HB, pp. 6-7.

It is against this severing of Being from thinking that the very center of Heidegger's attack is directed,[95] as we noted at the beginning of this chapter. It is in the light of this purpose that the hyperbolic statements, "We are still not thinking," and, "Science does not think" must be understood. Thought can be thought only so long as it lives in its element, Being.[96] Removed from this element, it is condemned to death.[97] In this seemingly unimportant separation of Being from thinking, then, we must see the fundamental attitude which has dominated our Western tradition since Plato.

We wish to understand the separation of Being and thinking in its source. It is the title for the fundamental posture of the Western spirit.[98]

The separation has had the effect of tearing thought away from its ground, Being as truth, of uprooting it and leaving it without foundation. But as long as the truth of Being is not thought, thought is without foundation.[99] The scientific and logico-mathematical thinking are valuable and perfectly valid ways of thinking,[100] but to assert that they are the *only* ways,[101] or that thought can be thought only so long as it conforms to their rules,[102] is to confuse the part with the whole. They are themselves in need of a more ultimate grounding, a grounding which they themselves cannot give.[103] Thus the thought which was attempted in SZ was called foundational thought[104] because it attempted to dig back to the foundation or ground of thought,[105] to penetrate to the very essence from which thought of Being in its truth derives.[106] It is only by digging back to this ultimate ground of thought, Being

---

[95] EM, p. 89.

[96] HB, p. 6.

[97] Thus Heidegger remarks in HB, p. 7: "Dieses geht zu Ende, wenn es aus seinem Element weicht. Das Element ist das, aus dem her das Denken vermag, ein Denken zu sein."

[98] "Wir wollen die Scheidung 'Sein und Denken' in ihrem Ursprung verstehen. Sie ist der Titel für die Grundhaltung des abendländischen Geistes." (EM, p. 111.) Cf. also EM, p. 89; VA, p. 231; WD, p. 103; and also Wiplinger, *Wahrheit und Geschichtlichkeit* ..., p. 346.

[99] HB, p. 41.

[100] DF, p. 122; WM, p. 13.

[101] EM, p. 92; Cf. also WM, p. 47.

[102] WM, pp. 47-48.

[103] DF, p. 8; EM, p. 93.

[104] WM, pp. 20-21.

[105] Concerning this point see for example Pöggeler, *Der Denkweg* ..., pp. 9, 47.

[106] HB, p. 41. Cf. also WM, pp. 9-10.

as φύσις-ἀλήθεια,[107] that the split between Being and thinking can be overcome.[108]

In trying to find this ultimate source of thought, therefore, Heidegger asks in the lectures of 1951-52, "*What* is thinking," "*Was* heisst Denken?" But in order to determine this, one must ask another, more basic question, what is it that calls thought forth, "Was *heisst* Denken?[109]

Thinking was not always understood as it is today.[110] As originally experienced in the period of its dawning and as expressed in the words of Parmenides[111] and Heraclitus,[112] it was a union of Being, ἐὸν ἔμμεναι φύσις, ἀλήθεια, λογος and νοεῖν.[113] The unity of thought and Being was expressed with a special clarity by Parmenides: χρὴ τὸ λέγειν τε νοεῖν τ' ἐὸν ἔμμεναι.[114] Need-ful is the gathered gathering which lets lie forth in openness (*Vorliegenlassen*), λέγειν, and the watchful care (*In-die-Acht-nehmen*), νοεῖν, of Being's, ἐὸν ἔμμεναι, revelation.[115] Both are needed, λέγειν,[116] the gathered gathering which lets lie forth in openness, and νοεῖν,[117] the apprehension of what has thus been made manifest. We must now determine the nature of νοεῖν, thinking, with which λέγειν is so closely connected, and the union of both with Being, since it is Being, which directs thought into its true nature as something belonging to it, and there preserves and guards it.[118]

The usual translation of νοεῖν as thinking is, at best, misleading,[119] since thinking is then understood and interpreted on the basis of our

[107] EM, p. 92.
[108] WM, pp. 9-10.
[109] WD, p. 83. On the four-fold usage of *heisst* see also WD, pp. 79-86, 150-153.
[110] WD, p. 105.
[111] WD, p. 119.
[112] EM, p. 110.
[113] WD, p. 148; EM, p. 78.
[114] For the extended examination of this text in WD, see pp. 108-149, 165-175; also EM, pp. 107, 129, 132.
[115] WD, p. 124.
[116] EM, p. 132.
[117] WD, p. 126.
[118] WD, pp. 147-148.
[119] Thus Heidegger remarks: "Dieses Wort (νοεῖν) bedeutet ursprünglich nicht 'denken' so wenig wie das λέγειν." (WD, p. 172.) Cf. also WD, pp. 119-120; EM, p. 107. Laffoucrière also remarks on the translation of νοεῖν by the word "thinking": "nous supposerions abusivement que l'Éléate traite déjà de la pensée comme d'une chose définie avec clarté. Il se situe seulement en plein exercice, en pleine manifestation — *Wesen* — en plein acte de penser. Ni *legein* pris pour soi, ni *noein* pris pour soi ne veulent dire: penser." (*Le Destin de la pensée* ..., p. 51.) Cf. also James Demske, *Sein, Mensch und Tod: Das Todesproblem bei Martin Heidegger* (München: Alber, 1963), pp. 98-99.

own experience of it[120] which represents a narrowing[121] of the meaning of thought[122] corresponding to its separation from Being. Its full richness can only be understood when all three are grasped in unity — χρή it is necessary,[123] not only that νοεῖν grow out of λέγειν,[124] but that both stand under the command (*Geheiss*) of Being and be directed to it and by it.[125]

Νοεῖν is translated by Heidegger as *vernehmen*, to apprehend or ac-cept. The apprehension, however, is to be understood in a twofold sense. It means, first of all, to accept, to let what shows itself come to one.[126] *Vernehmen* also means to hear a witness, to interrogate him with a view to determining how things stand.[127] Thus *vernehmen* is not to be understood in a purely passive way,[128] but also to take a receptive attitude toward it.[129] To use Heidegger's example, when troops prepare to "receive" the enemy, their hope, at the very least, is to bring them to a stand. Νοεῖν is to be understood in a similar way.[130] It is a receptive attitude which lets that which appears come forth and brings

---

[120] This is clear from Heidegger's remarks in WD, for example, p. 127: "Denn jetzt erklären die mittelalterliche und die neuzeitliche Philosophie das *griechische* Wesen von λέγειν und νοεῖν, von λογος und νοῦς aus *ihrem* Begriff der ratio her. Diese Erklärung klärt jedoch nicht mehr auf, sondern sie verdunkelt."

[121] WD, pp. 119-120, 92, 126, 172.

[122] WD, pp. 126, 172.

[123] WD, p. 119.

[124] WD, p. 127.

[125] WD, p. 148.

[126] EM, p. 105.

[127] EM, p. 105.

[128] Thus Heidegger points out that the νοεῖν is not just a passive "taking something in" when he notes: "Im νοεῖν waltet ein Vernehmen, das jedoch im voraus kein blosses Hinnehmen von etwas ist." (WD, p. 172.) Laffoucrière brings this point out very well, i.e. that the receptive attitude far from being pure passivity involves the whole manner of man's being open to the world and the world to man: "Faut-il identifier *noein* à percevoir? Peut-être mais pas au sens que prend le mot dans l'expression 'percevoir un bruit.' Rien de la 'réceptivité' que Kant attribuait à la perception sensible en contraste avec une 'spontanéité' de la raison. Le *percevoir* dont il s'agit n'est pas passif. Le *nous* est actif; il porte en lui le mouvement de s'occuper de quelque chose, il exprime l'action d'être attentif à quelque chose. Cette action du *Nous* consiste à méditer, à réfléchir sur, à interroger. En elle, quelque chose prend pour nous un sens, nous l'avons à cœur ... Par ce vocable est traduit non seulement ce que nous appelons aujourd'hui 'pensée,' mais toute activité humaine ... Il évoque d'une part l'ouverture de l'homme sur le monde à travers ses cinq sens. D'autre part, la signification de ce monde." (*Le Destin de la pensée* ..., p. 50.)

[129] EM, p. 105.

[130] EM, p. 105.

it to stand.[131] Νοεῖν is not simply a "faculty", e.g. reason, belonging to man or an immaterial activity of spirit[132] in virtue of which man is different from the lower animals not similarly endowed. It is, rather, a process by which Dasein first comes into Being, and hence into being himself,[133] as a human being.[134]

The "thinking," then, that is expressed in νοεῖν is as far removed as possible from thinking as the term is understood in a logico-scientific context.[135] This latter conceives of thinking in the Promethean terms of an active, aggressive assault upon Being.

From this there arises a completely new posture of man in the world and to the world. Now the world appears as an object toward which calculative thought directs its attack, which nothing can any longer withstand.[136]

For calculative thought Being is reduced to the status of an object[137] over-against man,[138] which can be reckoned up, to which man addresses himself in terms of "stand, and deliver."[139] Νοεῖν is, on the contrary, a receiving, but not simply a passive receiving. It takes to mind and heart what has come forth in revelation, there to guard and tend it.

What calls us to thought demands of itself that it be served, nurtured, and protected in its own essence through thought.[140]

Νοεῖν as *vernehmen*, then, is a "In-die-Acht-nehmen," a taking to mind and heart, a watchful guardianship[141] which stands at antipodes to a

---

[131] EM, p. 106.

[132] WD, p. 146.

[133] This point is brought out by Emmanuel Levinas in, *En découvrant l'existence avec Husserl et Heidegger* (Paris: Vrin, 1949), p. 59.

[134] EM, p. 108.

[135] WD, p. 154.

[136] "Daraus erwächst eine völlig neue Stellung des Menschen in der Welt und zur Welt. Jetzt erscheint die Welt wie ein Gegenstand, auf den das rechnende Denken seine Angriffe ansetzt, denen nichts mehr soll widerstehen können." (G, pp. 19-20.)

[137] HW, p. 85.

[138] G, p. 58; HW, p. 84. Cf. also Wiplinger, pp. 346-347.

[139] This point is brought out very clearly by Guilead: "L'attitude de la technique est provocante. Par elle, la façon de poser les choses et de se comporter envers les choses est totalement changée: elle ne porte même plus le caractère de la représentation objective, mais celui du commandement. Et les choses n'ont même plus le statut des objets, mais du fonds (Bestand)." *Le problème de la liberté chez Heidegger.* Cf. (Louvain: Nauwelaerts 1965), p. 89. Also VA, pp. 22-24.

[140] "Was uns denken heisst, verlangt von sich her, dass es durch das Denken in seinem eigenen Wesen bedient, gepflegt, behütet sei." (WD, p. 85.)

[141] WM, p. 49.

grasping, calculative approach to Being.[142] "Die Acht ist die Wacht,"[143] the taking to heart of Being is seen as a careful guarding and tending, such as the care-ful[144] solicitude which the shepherd has for his flock. Man is, as we have seen, the shepherd of Being. But the guardianship itself needs a guarding, and this is accomplished in the νοεῖν.[145] Thus we find in the saying of Parmenides the impersonal verb χρή, it is necessary, placed at the head of the sentence,[146] which indicates that the word is to receive primary emphasis. According to the rules of Greek grammar, an impersonal verb has the infinitive as its subject. Hence the three articular infinitives, τὸ λέγειν, τὸ νοεῖν, τ' ἐὸν ἔμμεναι are the subjects — what is needed. Λέγειν and νοεῖν, the letting lie forth in disclosure (*Vorliegenlassen*), and the taking to heart (*In-die-Acht-nehmen*) of what so lies forth in openness, are in service to Being and come to pass under its command.[147] To stress the reciprocal bond which exists between νοεῖν and λέγειν and ἐὸν ἔμμεναι, Parmenides does not simply link them by the ordinary conjunction καί, "and." Rather, the particle τε is employed, τε λέγειν, τε νοεῖν, τ' ἐὸν ἔμμεναι, which conveys the sense of reciprocity,[148] or mutuality.

It joins the λέγειν with the νοεῖν not simply with a mere καί, through an 'and,' but rather the saying reads: τε λεγειν τε νοεῖν τε. This τε-τε has a reflexive meaning and says: λέγειν and νοεῖν, allowing-to-lie-forth and the taking to heart pertain to each other and in each other, and indeed, reciprocally.[149]

[142] WD, p. 128.

[143] WD, 172.

[144] HD, pp. 25, 29.

[145] WD, p. 172.

[146] EM, p. 129.

[147] On Being's (ἐὸν ἔμμεναι) need for a cor-responding λέγειν-νοεῖν by man, Marx points out: "Als Ergebnis dieser Interpretation genügt es festzuhalten, dass das Geschehen der partizipialen Einheit der Differenz von Sein und Seiendem nicht als waltend hervor-kommen könnte (*aletheuein*), wenn es nicht die menschlichen Wesensweisen gäbe, die es 'vorliegen lassen' und es 'in die Acht nehmen.' Solch ein 'Vorliegenlassen' macht für Heidegger den Sinn des *legein*, legt dem strukturell zu ihm gehörigen *noein* das Geschehen der Differenz von Sein und Seiendem vor, so dass es von diesem 'in die Acht' genommen werden kann. In dieser Weise 'braucht' das *eon emmenai* das Wesen des Menschen." (*Heidegger und die Tradition* ..., p. 214.)

[148] This reciprocity between λέγειν and νοεῖν is brought out very clearly by Laffoucrière: "Ainsi le *legein* appelle le *noein* et à son tour, le *noein* renvoie au *legein* en un incessant mouvement circulaire." (*Le Destin de la pensée* ..., p. 51.)

[149] "Sie verknüpft nicht lediglich das λέγειν mit dem νοεῖν durch ein blosses καί, durch ein 'und,' sondern der Spruch lautet: τε λέγειν τε νοεῖν τε. Dieses τε-τε hat ein rückbezügliche Bedeutung und sagt: λέγειν und νοεῖν, Vorliegenlassen und In-die-Acht-nehmen gehen aufeinander und ineinander und zwar wechselweise." (WD, p. 126.)

The unity is not simply a unity of otherwise heterogeneous elements,[150] or of things alien to each other.[151] Rather there is a dynamic reciprocity[152] and com-penetration which constantly takes place, a kind of symbiosis. But although there is this dynamically resonating bond of reciprocity uniting them, still in the saying of Parmenides that we are considering the λέγειν is mentioned first.[153] The reason for this is because it is from λέγειν that νοεῖν first takes its essence as a *gathering* apprehension.

It remains to be asked why the λέγειν is named before the νοεῖν. The answer is that it is only from the λέγειν that the νοεῖν preserves its essence as a gathering apprehension.[154]

The taking into custody (*In-die-Acht-nehmen*) of what has come to appear is determined by λέγειν — "The νοεῖν, the taking to heart, is determined through the λέγειν".[155] This means that "νοεῖν unfolds out of λέγειν".[156] But if νοεῖν unfolds out of λέγειν, the taking (*nehmen*) of the apprehension (*vernehmen*) is not a grasping as is the case with calculative thought. On the contrary, it is a letting-come-forth of what lies before us — "The taking is not a laying hold of, but rather a letting come forth of that which lies forth."[157] It is a gathering (*In-die-Acht-nehmen*) of this manifestation of presencing (*Anwesen*), which in its turn must be gathered and guarded by λέγειν.[158]

According to Heidegger, therefore, the conjunction of λέγειν and νοεῖν and ἐὸν ἔμμεναι is the fundamental characteristic of thought.[159] In the ἐὸν ἔμμεναι is concealed that which calls thought into its essence.[160] It calls thought forth, directs it to its true nature,[161] and in such a way that thinking must always be oriented toward it and happens for its

---

[150] EM, p. 129.

[151] WD, p. 126.

[152] EM, p. 111.

[153] EM, p. 129.

[154] "Zu fragen bleibt, weshalb das λέγειν vor dem νοεῖν genannt ist. Die Antwort lautet: erst aus dem λέγειν erhält das νοεῖν sein Wesen als versammelndes Vernehmen." (EM, p. 129.)

[155] "Das νοεῖν, In-die-Acht-nehmen, wird durch das λέγειν bestimmt." (WD, p. 127.)

[156] "... das νοεῖν entfaltet sich vom λέγειν her." (WD, p. 127.)

[157] "Das Nehmen ist kein Zugreifen, sondern ein Ankommenlassen des Vorliegenden." (WD, p. 127.)

[158] WD, p. 125. Cf. also HW, p. 84.

[159] "Das Gefüge von λέγειν und νοεῖν ist der Grundzug des Denkens ..." (WD, p. 128.)

[160] WD, p. 149.

[161] HW, p. 83.

sake.[162] Thinking can be thinking only so long as it remains dependent on Being and directed toward it.[163] Only then will it live in its element, Being. Thinking is thinking *of* Being. The genitive usage is to be taken both as an objective and subjective genitive, i.e. in the objective sense thought must be focused on Being and rooted in it or it is groundless and without foundation; in the subjective sense, thought belongs to Being,[164] can only come into being as a result of the fecundating touch of Being. In a word, Being and thought belong together, not separated. The νοεῖν *as* νοεῖν belongs together with the εἶναι and thus belongs in the εἶναι itself."[165]

This unity of thought and Being found its expression in another fragment attributed to Parmenides which is of such fundamental import that it has become the basic theme of all Western thinking, as Heidegger interprets the history of philosophy.

... the saying τὸ γὰρ αὐτὸ νοεῖν ἔστιν τε καὶ εἶναι becomes the basic theme of all Western European thought.[166]

In the expression: τὸ γὰρ αὐτὸ νοεῖν ἔστιν τε καὶ εἶναι[167] the εἶναι has the same meaning as the ἐὸν ἔμμεναι of the fragment we have just considered — "εἶναι says ἐὸν ἔμμεναι ..."[168] What is of interest to us here is the unity of thought and Being, and this is expressed especially in the αὐτό. According to the rules of Greek grammar this word can have various meanings, demonstrative, as well as intensive and reflexive, depending on its position with respect to the word or words with which it is associated. Heidegger understands it to mean "the same," but not in the sense of "like in kind," or "identical."[169] It is to be taken rather in the sense of belonging together.[170] Being, εἶναι (or ἐὸν ἔμμεναι) and νοεῖν (*In-die-Acht-nehmen*) belong to each other, but in such a way that the individual identity of each is preserved.[171]

---

[162] EM, pp. 129, 135, 140.

[163] WD, p. 146.

[164] HB, p. 7. Cf. also WM, p. 47.

[165] "Das νοεῖν gehört *als* νοεῖν mit dem εἶναι zusammen und gehört so in das εἶναι selbst." (WD, p. 146.) Heidegger's emphasis.

[166] "... der Spruch τὸ γὰρ αὐτὸ νοεῖν ἔστιν τε καὶ εἶναι wird das Grundthema des gesammten abendländisch-europäischen Denkens." (WD, p. 148.) Cf. also EM, p. 111.

[167] WD, p. 146.

[168] "... εἶναι besagt ἐὸν ἔμμεναι ..." (WD, p. 147.)

[169] WD, p. 147.

[170] N, I, p. 528.

[171] EM, p. 108. In the τὸ αὐτό we must keep in mind all of the things that were

To answer the question *what* is thinking (*was* heisst Denken), another question must first be answered[172] what calls thinking forth (was *heisst* Denken). It is the call (*Geheiss*) of Being which e-vokes thought,[173] determines it to be what it is, and keeps and preserves it in its true essence.[174] It is the profound and intimate unity between ἐὸν ἔμμεναι λέγειν and νοεῖν which constitutes the authentic essence of thought.[175]

From these considerations several points have emerged which are of importance to us for Heidegger's critique of logic. First as far as the logic problematic is concerned, the very center of his attack is directed against the severing of Being from thinking. Second, thinking which has been severed from its vitalizing union with Being is not thinking at all, at least in the plenary Heideggerian understanding of the word. Third, the essential foundation of thought is Being as truth, φύσις-ἀλήθεια. Fourth, Heidegger's critique of logic must be situated within what is for him a larger question, the problem of thought — what type of thinking is an adequate response to Being as truth? Clearly this is not the thinking for Heidegger, that has been treated under the traditional rubric of logic.[176]

---

said of λόγος as ἕν-πάντα, that is, a binding together into unity of elements which strive to separate. In this connection Demske points out: "... was heisst τὸ αὐτό? Nicht Identität im Sinne der Einerleiheit, Selbigkeit oder blossen Gleichgültigkeit, sondern vielmehr Zusammengehörigkeit des Gegenstrebigen, im Sinne des Parmenideischen ἕν und des Heraklitischen λόγος bzw. πόλεμος." (*Sein, Mensch und Tod* ..., p. 98.)

[172] WD, p. 160.

[173] WD, p. 146.

[174] WD, p. 148.

[175] WD, p 139.

[176] For a fuller treatment of thinking as νοεῖν see my article, "Heidegger: Thinking as *NOEIN*," *Modern Schoolman*, LI (1973), 17-28.

CHAPTER V

SYMBOLIC LOGIC:
ITS DEVELOPMENT AND RELATION TO TECHNICITY

Thus far on a number of occasions we have touched upon Heidegger's
reconstruction of the history of philosophy, according to which an event
of momentous consequences took place in the thought of Plato, i.e.
the essence of truth as ἀλήθεια was lost and replaced by the Platonic
Idea, ἰδέα. It was this changed notion of truth which made possible
the birth and development of logic. It is to this, the origin of logic
and its evolution into symbolic or mathematical logic that we now turn
our attention. As Heidegger viewed the history of philosophy, one of
the crucial moments of the Western tradition took place in the thought
of Plato, and particularly in Book VII of the *Republic* in the allegory
of the cave.[1] Here a change in the notion of truth took place,
the importance of which we have yet to grasp, according to Heidegger.
Truth, which had originally been experienced by the great Pre-Socratic
thinkers as ἀλήθεια, an unveiling which also tends toward concealment,
now finds its expression in the thought of Plato as ἰδέα. The noun ἰδέα
is related, etymologically, to the verb ἰδεῖν,[2] which means to see or
perceive. Thus truth, now expressed as ἰδέα no longer has the sense
of a process of revelation, but rather comes to take on the meaning
of a static presence which is seen. From this point in history forward,
the essence of truth will no longer be unhiddenness, but will be determined
by correctness of perception,[3] and statement about what is perceived.
Henceforth, the standard of truth will be agreement, ὁμοίωσις,[4] between
perceiving and the thing perceived. Truth now becomes correctness,
ὀρθότης.[5] As a consequence of the change in the essence of truth,

---

[1] PL, p. 33.
[2] PL, p. 42.
[3] PL, pp. 35, 41, 42, 43.
[4] PL, p. 42. Cf. also EM, p. 141.
[5] PL, p. 42. Cf. also WD, p. 14; EM, p. 144.

the locus of truth also changes.[6] The seat of truth now becomes the assertion.[7] The ἰδέα is something to be seen,[8] an object which confronts one, something to be looked at, and hence separated from the beholder.[9] Truth, then, becomes a correctness of vision, a *correspondence* of seeing with the object beheld, and a correctness of statement about it. In all this, however, Being as a process of revelation, ἀλήθεια has been forgotten.[10]

With Aristotle, as the forgetfulness of Being deepens, λόγος (and its correlate λέγειν), originally Being in its collectedness which makes possible self-manifestation,[11] is reduced to assertions,[12] λέγειν τι κατά τινος to say something of something else, viz. the proposition.[13] Since the development of knowledge about the proposition is a necessary pre-condition for the development of logic, and since the transformation of truth as ἀλήθεια into ἰδέα is the necessary pre-condition for the development of the proposition, it is clear that logic owes its birth to the forgetfulness of Being as truth.[14]

Truth, with Aristotle, becomes a property of the proposition.[15] Its locus is in the mind, not, as formerly, a process inseparable from beings themselves by which they are lit up and revealed in their presence.[16] Thus Aristotle states that truth and falsity are properly in the mind of man, not things.[17] Truth is formally found in the judgment act;[18] the judgment is true when it corresponds to the thing to which it refers.[19] As Heidegger sees it, it is this notion of truth as correspondence which has governed Western philosophy since Plato.[20] This teaching of Aristotle is taken over by the middle ages and expressed in the well-known scholastic definition of truth — "veritas est adaequatio intellectus et rei",

[6] PL, p. 42.
[7] PL, p. 44; EM, p. 142.
[8] ZS, pp. 15-16.
[9] EM, p. 48.
[10] PL, pp. 44-45; EM, pp. 144-145.
[11] EM, pp. 141-142.
[12] EM, p. 44.
[13] WD, p. 100; EM, p. 142; DF, p. 119.
[14] EM, pp. 91-93, 130-131, 143.
[15] EM, p. 142.
[16] EM, p. 142.
[17] PL, p. 44.
[18] DF, p. 113.
[19] DF, p. 91; WD, p. 14.
[20] EM, pp. 137-138, 141, 144; N, II, p. 220; PL, p. 49; SZ, pp. 214-215.

a correspondence between the mind and the object of thought.[21] It is properly found only in the mind.

The statement of Thomas Aquinas holds true for medieval scholasticism in general: Veritas proprie invenitur in intellectu humano vel divino (Questiones de Veritate; ques. I, art. 4, resp.), "truth is properly found in the intellect, either human or divine." It has its essential place in the understanding.[22]

With the advent of Descartes, philosophy moves into a new and decisive phase.[23] In Heidegger's eyes, he,[24] together with Hegel[25] and Nietzsche,[26] are the three consummators of metaphysics, drawing Plato's thought to its ultimate possibilities. Thus the wedge which was driven between Being and thought by Plato when Being was conceived as ἰδέα, something to be seen or contemplated,[27] receives an additional, and decisive, thrust from Descartes.[28] Man is now conceived as a subject,[29] the world as objects,[30] and an unbridgeable gulf has been created between them. Thought becomes the activity of a subject re-presenting (repraesentatio, vor-stellen)[31] objects (Gegen-stände).[32] Here we should note carefully that Heidegger wishes the words vor-stellen, set-before, and Gegen-stand, ob-ject, stand-against, to have their full etymological meaning.[33] Post-Cartesian thought will be of such a sort that a sub-ject pro-posed to itself ob-jects which stand-over-against it.[34]

Moving beyond Descartes, as Western metaphysics unfolds it evolves into the thought of Kant, who, according to Heidegger, has a pivotal place in the history of philosophy, reflecting as he does the after-glow of the greatness of the early Greeks, and pointing forward to the speculative idealism of the next century.[35] Heidegger sees a marked similarity in purpose between his own work and that of Kant. In the

[21] DF, p. 91; PL, p. 26; SZ, p. 214.
[22] PL, pp. 44-45.
[23] HW, p. 91.
[24] HW, p. 91.
[25] EM, pp. 137, 144; WD, p. 146; VA, p. 76; SG, pp. 114, 145-146. Hereafter, SG.
[26] PL, pp. 37, 50; HW, pp. 193-196, 234, 242-246; N, II, pp. 201, 291-302.
[27] EM, p. 138.
[28] HW, pp. 80, 91.
[29] US, p. 248.
[30] HW, p. 85; EM, p. 104.
[31] HW, p. 84; KTS, p. 12.
[32] HW, p. 102.
[33] KT, p. 22; HW, p. 85.
[34] KT, p. 16.
[35] KT, p. 36.

Kritik der reinen Vernunft, Kant was attempting to establish the foundations of metaphysics, as was Heidegger in *Sein und Zeit*.[36] In addition, Kant in the *Kritik* sets limits to a purely rationalist metaphysics, a metaphysics which concerns itself solely with the manipulation of concepts, and stresses the role of intuition in human knowledge.[37] Heidegger, for his part, also sets limits to a purely rationalist metaphysics, dominated by logic.

However, in spite of Kant's greatness, he remains within the tradition of the forgetfulness of Being as ἀλήθεια,[38] as we shall see. In the development of Western philosophy following Descartes, reason had established itself, on its own authority, as the supreme tribunal from which all judgment upon the nature of things was to be passed.[39] Prior to Descartes, indeed beginning with Plato and Aristotle, λόγος was transformed into an ὄργανον, or tool.[40] The originally experienced λόγος was changed into *ratio*, and the stage was set for the dominance of this same reason, (*ratio*).[41] Truth by the time of the Scholastics had become an affair of the mind. After Descartes, with the establishment of man as subject and the conception of thought as his re-presenting of objects,[42] thought became even farther separated from Being. By the time of Kant, this movement, initiated by Plato and Aristotle and given a decisively added impetus by Descartes, had reached the point of exhaustion. Metaphysics had degenerated into a purely formal exercise, manipulating foundationless and empty concepts according to the rules of Aristotelian logic. Kant therefore attempted to set limits to this formalism in the *Kritik*, stressing the necessity of intuition in cognition — thought had, somehow, to make its way back over to its object.

In the beginning, Kant could, according to Heidegger, take over the existing logic[43] which purported to be the doctrine of thought,[44]

---

[36] Thus Heidegger remarks in HB, p. 41, concerning his purpose in SZ: "Solange jedoch die Wahrheit des Seins nicht gedacht ist, bleibt alle Ontologie ohne ihr Fundament. Deshalb bezeichnete sich das Denken, das mit 'S. U. Z.' in die Wahrheit des Seins vorzudenken versuchte, als Fundamentalontologie.

[37] DF, p. 115.

[38] KT, p. 36.

[39] EM, pp. 147-418.

[40] EM, p. 143; HW, p. 287. Compare also KT, pp. 34-35.

[41] EM, p. 136, 147-148.

[42] VA, p. 234.

[43] SZ, p. 215; DF, p. 117; VA, pp. 141-142.

[44] DF, p. 113; EM, p. 91.

but with the reservation that this thought must be related to intuition.[45] The remnant of the original λόγος of which Kant was the inheritor had by now been reduced to a representation of logical relations.[46] The λόγος is merely a judgment which fits together objects of thought into a certain unity.[47] This judgment was, as it seemed to Kant, not incorrect, but had to be rejected as inadequate. Heidegger remarks on this point:

> What Kant here rejects as inadequate is precisely the definition of Meier, i.e. of Baumgarten and Wolff. What is meant is the definition of judgment as assertion, commonly accepted in logic since Aristotle, λέγειν τι κατά τινος. Kant, however, does not say that this definition is false; he says merely that it is unsatisfactory.[48]

Thus underlying the pure reason which is set within limits by the *Kritik* is the λόγος of Aristotle.

"Pure" reason is to be understood as reason in its self-asserted claim to be the court of last resort in human knowledge,[49] in its self-proclaimed authority in the determination of the nature of things,[50] as a special form of the drive toward mathematization,[51] i.e. to skip over the things themselves and to determine the Being of things out of pure thought. It is for this "pure reason" that Kant wishes to set limits, for this is, indeed, the sense of the *Kritik*, i.e. a study of the nature and structure of reason and the establishment of appropriate limits, dictated by its nature and structure.[52] The rationalist metaphysics which was prevalent at the time of Kant took knowledge to be purely conceptual thought. It is this which must be deprived of its presumed superiority and its claim of exclusivity. Thought must have intuition as its foundation,[53] and indeed thought must serve intuition.[54]

Traditional metaphysics, for its part, had claimed a knowledge of being through pure concepts,[55] that is, by thought alone.[56] The essence, structure, and rules of operation of this thought had been set forth

---

[45] DF, p. 117.
[46] DF, p. 121.
[47] DF, pp. 121-122.
[48] DF, p. 121.
[49] DF, p. 83.
[50] DF, p. 92.
[51] DF, p. 83.
[52] DF, p. 96. Cf. also SG, p. 125.
[53] DF, p. 114.
[54] DF, p. 116.
[55] DF, p. 186.
[56] KM, p. 107.

and limited by general logic.[57] "Pure thought" is the fitting together of concepts, in the judgment.[58] It is purely explicative of what is represented in the judgment and does not arrive at new knowledge. Here, "we have merely played with representations".[59] The judgment so understood is merely a connecting of representations,[60] e.g. "all bodies are extended". The understanding is the power of binding together representations[61] which have been formed by it. This characterization of the judgment and proposition as a mere connecting of representations of the understanding is not rejected by Kant because it is incorrect, but is rejected as being an inadequate account of human knowledge.[62] In Heidegger's view, and this point is important, it is this understanding of the proposition as a mere connection of concepts that became the basis of what has developed into symbolic or mathematical logic, or as Heidegger usually designates it, logistics (*Logistik*).[63] This term *Logistik* we shall translate usually as symbolic or mathematical logic unless otherwise noted, since these terms are more normally used in English.

General logic, then, sets forth the rules which govern the inferences, the laws of unitability of purely conceptual representations.[64] It is concerned with *entia rationis*, beings of the mind, as the Scholastics had called them. Within this isolated conceptual realm the first principle is the Principle of Contradiction. To be unitable in a judgment the concepts may not contradict one another.[65] But mere unitability of subject and predicate only says that the assertion, λέγειν τι κατά τινος,

---

[57] KM, p. 107.

[58] KM, p. 107.

[59] KM, p. 107.

[60] DF, p. 122.

[61] DF, p. 122.

[62] DF, p. 122.

[63] Heidegger, following the usage on the continent, understands this term broadly to mean "symbolic logic", "mathematical logic" or "mathematics applied to propositions". Cf. DF, p. 122. On the meaning of this term, Carnap notes: "In addition to 'symbolic logic' and 'mathematical logic', the designation 'logistics' is often used, especially on the European continent; it is short and permits the formulation of the adjective 'logistic'. The word 'logistics' originally signified the art of reckoning, and was proposed by Couturat, Itelson and Lalande independently in 1904 as a name for symbolic logic ...". *Introduction To Symbolic Logic and Its Applications*, trans. W. Meyer and J. Wilkinson (New York: Dover, 1958), p. 3.

[64] DF, p. 145.

[65] DF, p. 134; KM, p. 108; WD, p. 100.

is possible in so far as no contradiction hinders it.[66] It does not reach the sphere of the essence of judgment, or take into consideration an object relationship. Freedom from contradiction tells so little about the judgment that it may still be false or even meaningless.[67] The Principle of Contradiction is, then, quite obviously not the supreme principle of human knowledge.

The analytic judgment which merely remains in the conceptual order, which concerns itself solely with the subject-predicate relationship as such prescinds from any relationship of the judgment to an object.[68] This remnant of λόγος, the assertion, divested of all relation to objects, is the concern of general logic.[69] The assertion is understood "logically", that is, as a being of the mind, an *ens rationis*. The understanding is also taken "logically", that is, as the power of coupling its representations.[70] It is this conception of the assertion and understanding that Kant rejects as inadequate[71] according to Heidegger.

As Kant sees it, the pure thought of metaphysics which lays claim to knowing Being by concepts is not knowledge itself, but only one element of knowledge.[72] An adequate account of knowledge must take into consideration the relationship of the assertion to the things to which it refers,[73] since it is the thing which is the determining factor in knowledge.[74] Knowledge, therefore, must "go beyond" a "pure thought", isolated in itself, and make its way over to its object. This relation to what is other than pure thought, i.e. beings, Kant terms synthesis,[75] and it is only through synthetic judgments, judgments that make their way over to the object that we have an adequate account of human knowledge.[76] Kant's distinction between analytic and synthetic judgment, according to Heidegger, indicates nothing less than a changed conception of the λόγος and all that pertains to it, i.e. the logical.[77] The "logical" up to the time of Kant had been limited to the connection and

[66] DF, p. 134; EM, p. 143.
[67] DF, p. 134.
[68] DF, p. 139.
[69] DF, p. 137.
[70] DF, p. 145.
[71] DF, p. 145.
[72] KM, p. 108.
[73] DF, pp. 145-146.
[74] KM, p. 108.
[75] KM, p. 108.
[76] DF, pp. 137-138.
[77] DF, p. 125.

relation of concepts.[78] Kant's new definition of the logical insists that
the "logical" is not merely a relation of concepts to each other but
that the "logical" must take into account the entire structure of the
judgment as it is established in advance from its relations to the object
and the human knower.[79] In this scheme of things, intuition will play
a central role. The judgment act must be essentially directed toward
intuition.[80] Thinking must be united to intuition and serve it. Through
such a union or synthesis, thought is referred to the object, which in
the unity of a thinking intuition, is known.[81]

This means that there is a structural unity of three elements in
the cognitive process, i.e. intuition, transcendental imagination, and
understanding.[82] Of these three elements, the transcendental imagination
is the structural center.[83] Here it is outside the scope of our purpose
to enter into the question of the changed function of the transcendental
imagination in the second edition of the *Kritik*,[84] and the two Heidegger
interpretations, *Kant und das Problem der Metaphysik* (1929) based on
the first edition, and *Die Frage nach dem Ding* (1962) based on the
second.[85] What is important for our purpose is to note simply that
thought must be rooted in intuition and must necessarily depend on it.[86]
Thought is in the service of intuition.[87]

In this synthetic judgment of Kant, then, we have a new definition
of judgment.[88] Judgment as an action of understanding is not only
related to intuition and object, but its essence is defined from this
relation and even as this relation.[89] From this a new concept of
understanding also arises. Understanding is now no longer merely a
faculty of connecting mental representations[90] but is in dynamic synthesis

[78] DF, p. 125.
[79] DF, p. 125.
[80] DF, pp. 114-115.
[81] KM, p. 109.
[82] KM, p. 109.
[83] KM, p. 64.
[84] KM, p. 220.
[85] For a detailed study of this question, see William Richardson, "Kant and the
Later Heidegger", *Phenomenology in America* ..., pp. 125-144; also, Ingeborg Koza,
Das Problem des Grundes in Heideggers Auseinandersetzung mit Kant ..., pp. 31-33.
[86] KM, p. 76.
[87] DF, p. 115.
[88] DF, p. 123.
[89] DF, p. 123.
[90] DF, p. 123.

78 SYMBOLIC LOGIC

with intuition through the transcendental imagination.[91] The rationalist metaphysical tradition had determined the Being of things out of pure thought.[92] The essential structure of the object as a bearer of attributes was interpreted according to the structure of the proposition, as a unity of subject and predicate.[93] For Kant, however, pure thought cannot be the final court of appeal for the determination of the object.[94] Logic, in the sense of general logic, cannot be the basic science of metaphysics.[95] According to Kant's newly transformed definition of the essence of thought and judgment, the essence of logic must also be changed.[96] The general logic which had been dominant and which was concerned simply with the relation and connection of concepts with each other must give place to a logic which takes account of the relation to the object of knowledge through intuition.[97] This logic is not the traditional formal logic, but rather a logic which is determined from the synthetic unity of apperception.[98] This logic is called "transcendental" logic.[99] It receives this designation because it concerns "transcendence", i.e. a thought which "passes over" to the object, is directed to the object, and deals with the relation of "passing over" as such.[100]

Thus in Kant's transcendental logic we have a magnificent effort to overcome the radical split between being and thinking. In the final analysis, however, at least as Heidegger views Kant, Kant remains within the tradition of the forgetfulness of Being as truth and the subject-ism of Descartes.[101] Being has now become pure pos-ition[102] by the knowing subject;[103] the subject-ism of Descartes is only transposed to the tran-

---

[91] KM, p. 76; KT, p. 20.

[92] DF, p. 186.

[93] DF, p. 137.

[94] "... das blosse Denken kann nicht der Gerichtshof für die Bestimmung der Dingheit des Dinges sein, Kantisch gesprochen: für die Gegenständlichkeit des Gegenstandes." (DF, p. 137.)

[95] "Die Logik kann nicht die Grundwissenschaft der Metaphysik sein." (DF, p. 137.)

[96] "Gemäss der gewandelten Wesensbestimmung von Denken und Urteilen muss sich jedoch auch das Wesen der darauf bezogenen Logik wandeln ..." (DF, pp. 137-138.) Cf. also DF, 117.

[97] DF, pp. 145-146.

[98] KT, p. 20.

[99] DF, p. 138.

[100] DF, p. 138.

[101] KT, p. 36.

[102] KT, p. 16. Cf. also VA, p. 184.

[103] KT, p. 22.

scendental level.[104] The basically mathematical character of modern metaphysics, i.e. the determination in advance of the Being of things from conceptual principles, is retained.[105] It will be this latter point, that is, the essentially mathematical character of modern thought and its results to which we shall now turn our attention.

In Heidegger's view, modern natural science, modern mathematics and modern metaphysics have all sprung from the same root — the mathematizing tendency of the human mind.[106] Modern thought in general has as its foundation the "mathematical" (*das Mathematische*).[107] To characterize all of modern thought as basically "mathematical" seems, at least at first glance, a curious contention. In order to see why Heidegger should be led to make such assertions, we must now try to understand what he means by the "mathematical" (*das Mathematische*), and how it happens that it has become the foundation of modern thought. When the term "mathematical" is used, one would ordinarily associate it with something having to do with numbers.[108] The "mathematical" as Heidegger understands it, however, should be grasped in terms of causes which lie much deeper than the mathematical itself.[109] His concern, then, in reflecting on the nature of the mathematical is to attempt to grasp its metaphysical import.[110] Numbers, Heidegger would concede, which we ordinarily associate with the mathematical, are obviously related to it. But they are not to be identified with it. They are, rather, only the most obvious instance of it,[111] and since the most familiar example of it, we tend to identify them with the mathematical itself.[112] The essence of the mathematical, however, as Heidegger understands it, does not lie in numbers,[113] nor indeed in mathematics itself. Mathematics, too, if it is to be seen in terms of its most basic causes, is only a particular form of the mathematizing power of the mind.[114] For a clarification of the "mathematical" (*das Mathe-*

[104] SG, p. 148; KT, p. 20.

[105] DF, p. 95.

[106] DF, p. 75.

[107] Thus Heidegger remarks, "... der Grundzug des neuzeitlichen Denkens und Wissens im eigentlichen Sinne mathematisch ist". (DF, p. 59.)

[108] DF, p. 54.

[109] DF, p. 74.

[110] DF, p. 74.

[111] DF, p. 54.

[112] DF, p. 58.

[113] DF, p. 58.

[114] DF, p. 53.

matische) Heidegger returns to the Greek root-word from which it is derived, τὰ μαθήματα, that which has been learned or can be learned[115] Τὰ μαθήματα is itself based upon the verb μανθάνειν, to learn, as is μάθησις, which has both the sense of learning and that which is taught.[116] Hence, at least initially, these words were not identified with the science of quantitative measurement. For Heidegger then, τὰ μαθήματα had the sense of something already learned,[117] i.e. something known in advance.[118] Thus, in our daily dealing with the things of our experience before we can know bodies as bodies, we must somehow previously have a notion of "bodilyness"; before we can know plants or animals we must first have a notion of "plantness" and "animalness".[119] The mathematical is, therefore, what is known in advance of our contact with the thing.[120] Numbers, too, are an example of the mathematical.[121] For example, when we see three apples on the table, we *re*-cognize that there are three. But to do this we must previously have grasped what threeness is in order to be able to *re*-cognize that this is an instance of it.[122] But since number represents the most obvious example of the mathematical, i.e. the already-known-in-advance, we have come to identify the mathematical with the numerical.[123] The essence of the mathematical, however, does not lie in the numerical,[124] but rather the mathematical is the known-in-advance which makes knowledge of a given thing, as that kind of thing, possible.

We have seen now in a general way, what Heidegger understands by the "mathematical". As noted above, Heidegger contends that modern thought in general, and modern science in particular, is essentially "mathematical". In order to see why he should be led to such a conclusion, let us examine, at least in outline form, the procedure which is typically followed by modern sciences. Their method of procedure is basically this: observation, hypothesis, confirmation, law.[125] There

---

[115] DF, p. 53.
[116] DF, p. 53.
[117] DF, p. 53.
[118] DF, p. 58.
[119] HW, p. 72.
[120] HW, pp. 71-72.
[121] HW, p. 72.
[122] HW, p. 72.
[123] HW, p. 72.
[124] HW, p. 72.
[125] Cf. for example the classical statement of this by Sir James Jeans, *The New Background of Science* (New York: Macmillan, 1933), pp. 45-46.

is first of all observation of certain related phenomena, which are duly noted in protocal statements.[126] There is next a projected hypothesis of what the explanation might be that would account for all of the facts in the most satisfactory and economical way. There follows a series of experiments, or controlled experiences by which the hypothesis might be tested and thus confirmed or invalidated.[127] But before observation can take place it is clear that we must know in advance what we are looking for. The mathematical project (*der mathematische Entwurf*) which Heidegger has in mind is, then, a kind of ground plan or blue print of the structure of things which is sketched out in advance,[128] which makes possible the first protocal statements of the science. The mathematical project is a kind of surveying or laying out of the horizon within which things may appear.[129] As a surveying or laying of limits only those things may appear, and only those aspects of the things which are prefigured in the project.[130] Thus because of a distinctly different project animals will be meaningful to the micro-biologist in a totally different way than to the zoologist, and only those aspects of the animal will be meaningful to the micro-biologist which are given in the project in advance. Thus, in Heidegger's view, modern science's urge for experimentation and consequent claim of dealing only with things that are indubitable facts because established by experiment is, in reality, a result of skipping over the facts to begin with.[131] Rather than let the beings manifest themselves to thought, they are submitted

---

[126] We cannot here enter into the controverted question of "protocol language" and "physical language". See for example, R. Carnap, *The Unity of Science* (London: Kegan Paul, Trench, Trubner, 134), p. 81 ff; also *The Philosophy of Rudolf Carnap* ed. P. A. Schlipp (London: Cambridge Univ. Press, 1963), pp. 32, 93, 114, 199, 178-281. Here we are taking protocol statement in its simplest meaning; statements which record the empirical phenomena in the positive sciences e.g. chemistry, physics, etc.

[127] I. M. Bochenski, trans. P. Caws *The Methods of Contemporary Thought* (Dordrecht: Reidel, 1965), p. 98. Cf. also DF, pp. 66-74.

[128] "Der mathematische Entwurf ist ... der Vorausgriff in das Wesen der Körper; damit wird im *Grundriss* vorgezeichnet, wie jedes Ding und jede Beziehung jedes Dinges zu jedem Ding gebaut ist." (DF, p. 71.) Heidegger's emphasis.

[129] This is clear from the following statement. "Das Mathematische ist, als mente concipere, ein über die Dinge gleichsam hinwegspringender *Entwurf* ihrer Dingheit. Der Entwurf eröffnet erst einen Spielraum, darin die Dinge d.h. die Tatsachen, sich zeigen." (DF, p. 71.) Heidegger's emphasis.

[130] Cf. for example the following important text. "Wie sie sich zeigen, ist durch den Entwurf vorgezeichnet; er bestimmt deshalb auch die Weise des Hinnehmens und der Erkundung des sich Zeigenden, die Erfahrung, das experiri." (DF, p. 72.)

[131] DF, p. 72.

to an interrogation in which the type of answer which will be received is determined in advance by the conditions laid down in the questioning to which they are subjected.[132] The essence of the modern experiment is that it is a *controlled* experience. The beings in question can manifest themselves through their activity in only one way, the way that the experimenter has predetermined is meaningful for him.[133] The nature of our experience will be controlled and limited by the project since it pre-determines which experiences will be meaningful for a given project. Here the word experience is to be understood in the sense of the experience derived from experiment, i.e. a controlled experience.[134] Thus to test the hypothesis that a gas has certain properties, e.g. that its volume will increase upon heating, diminish with cooling, liquify if cooled sufficiently, undergo an increase in pressure if the volume remains constant and heat is introduced into the system, etc., the scientist will submit the gas in question to a series of controlled tests in which certain variables in the system, e.g. volume, temperature, can be changed while other elements are held constant. *Control* is obviously of the essence here; the being in question can manifest itself only in certain rigidly predetermined ways. The hypothesis is thus confirmed and becomes a law, and if it is wide enough to embrace within its explanation sufficiently diverse phenomena it is called a theory. An example of this may be seen in the formulation and subsequent verification of the theory of relativity. One of the mathematico-physical theories which served for the derivation of astronomical laws in the Copernican system was Newton's theory of gravitation. In 1915, Einstein proposed another theory, relativity, which had the greater merit of simplicity, reducing gravitation to purely geometric properties.[135] On the basis of his theory, Einstein had predicted that a light ray passing near a large mass would be deflected.[136] On May 29, 1919, there was an eclipse of the sun which occurred under especially favorable circumstances. An expedition to Principe in the Gulf of Guinea led by the English physicist Sir Arthur

---

[132] DF, p. 72.

[133] DF, p. 72.

[134] This is quite clear in the description provided by the noted scientist Sir Arthur Eddington, in *The Mathematical Principles of Relativity* (Cambridge: Cambridge Univ. Press, 1960), pp. 1-3.

[135] Eddington, *Mathematical Principles of Relativity* ..., pp. 81-82.

[136] Albert Einstein, *The Meaning of Relativity* (Princeton: Princeton Univ. Press, 1955), p. 93.

Eddington[137] was able to observe and verify the predictions which had been projected on the basis of the new theory, and thus the theory had its confirmation.[138]

Heidegger sees a particularly significant example of the mathematical project in Newton's first laws of motion.[139] Prior to Newton (and Galileo) the Aristotelian view of nature had held sway, i.e. nature was conceived of as an inner capacity of a body, determining its form of motion and place.[140] With Newton nature becomes the field of uniform space-time within which motion takes place and which is outlined in advance in the mathematical project.[141] It is only within the context of space-time-motion that bodies may appear.[142] Things now show themselves *only* in the relations of places and time points and in the measure of mass and work forces.[143]

Implied in this first law of motion is a revolution in which the concept of nature has changed completely, as well as man's relation to it. Consequently, the manner of questioning nature has also changed drastically.[144] This changed way of conceiving of nature has its source in Descartes' *cogito-sum*, in which man as ego-subject is related to his world as to an object. The program of mathematics and the experiment are based upon this relation of man as ego to the thing as object.[145] The world is seen as something calculable; science as a calculating and measuring investigation[146] which alone furnishes the key to its mystery.[147] The mathematical strives out of itself to establish its own essence as the ground of itself, and thus of all knowledge.[148] It takes

[137] See Eddington's very interesting description of the expedition given in *Mathematical Principles of Relativity* ..., p. 91.

[138] On verification through the observable results of experimentation, and the priority of the mathematical project over empirically observed phenomena, see Heidegger's interpretation of Galileo's celebrated experiment at Pisa, DF, pp. 69-70.

[139] DF, pp. 66-68.

[140] DF, p. 69.

[141] DF, p. 71.

[142] DF, p. 72.

[143] DF, p. 72.

[144] DF, p. 68.

[145] Thus Heidegger remarks in G, p. 58: "Der Mathematische Entwurf und das Experiment gründen in der Beziehung des Menschen als Ich zum Ding als Gegenstand."

[146] DF, p. 52.

[147] HH, p. 23.

[148] "Gemäss diesem inneren Zug ... drängt das Mathematische aus sich dazu, sein eigenes Wesen als Grund seiner selbst und somit *allen Wissens zu legen*." (DF, p. 75.) My emphasis.

itself for the *only* approach to nature. Heidegger suggests that the mathematical method of modern science is not merely one element among others in the sciences,[149] but rather that it plays a decisive role, since the mathematical project determines in advance what can become an object.[150] Further, the method of modern science, that is, how it pursues its object, decides beforehand what truth it will yield.[151]

From this brief description of the methodology of modern science, it should be clear that science in its development is inescapably dependent upon logic, and this for several reasons.[152] First, since in the physical sciences the acquisition of knowledge is in most cases indirect, that is, inferential, formal logic is an indispensable presupposition of scientific research. Second, while science remains in a primitive state of development "natural logic" is perhaps sufficient, but when science becomes highly developed, extremely complicated and abstract, this no longer suffices. Because science is *exact*, it needs an *exact* language.[153] Everyday language, words, and syntax are, for better or worse, filled with imprecisions, ambiguities, and exceptions.[154] Hence, in an exact science these elements must be eliminated as far as is humanly possible. Thus, in logic and the sciences there is a drive toward mathematization and, as a consequence of this, toward formalization of both thought and language. There are several reasons for this. First, because the concepts required are so abstract, it is impossible to find suitable words in ordinary language to express them.[155] The scientist, then, requires new, easily manipulatable symbols.[156] Second, the syntax of ordinary language is inexact and filled with exceptions and hence does not furnish the guarantee of exactness in usage required by science. Third, since the words of ordinary language have many meanings and nuances, they are, therefore, ambiguous and do not insure exactness.[157] Hence their extrusion from scientific

[149] DF, p. 79.

[150] DF, p. 79.

[151] DF, p. 79.

[152] In this connection see Susanne Langer's remarks in *Symbolic Logic* (New York: Dover, 1953), pp. 332-333.

[153] Werner Heisenberg, *Physics and Philosophy* (New York: Harper, 1958), pp. 171-172.

[154] Heisenberg, *Physics ...*, pp. 168-169.

[155] Heisenberg, *Physics ...*, pp. 178-179.

[156] Carnap, *Introduction to Symbolic Logic ...*, p. 2.

[157] Alfred Tarski, trans. J. Woodger, *Logic, Semantics, Metamathematics* (Oxford: Oxford at Clarendon Press, 1956), p. 60.

language and replacement by a symbol of univocal meaning is not only advantageous, but necessary.[158]

From this, it should be clear that the development of logic must also proceed in terms of mathematization and formalization if it is to be a fruitful instrument in the elaboration of science.[159] The movement in this direction Heidegger calls "logistics" (*Logistik*),[160] that is, symbolic or mathematical logic. With the help of mathematical methods one may calculate the system of connectives between assertions,[161] and hence it is designated "mathematical logic".[162] In Heidegger's view, however, for reasons we shall see, this is anything but logic.[163] It is merely mathematics applied to propositional forms.[164]

Symbolic/mathematical logic, in order to achieve the precision required by modern science, must utilize formalism. Space does not permit us to enter into all of the details of the process of formalization, but in outline its method is as follows.[165] The first step of the procedure is to choose certain symbols for the system. The symbols are considered *only* as symbols, that is, the logician prescinds from their *meaning*, and regards only their *form*.[166] For the operations of the logician, the sign is emptied of meaning,[167] so to say. Attention is directed away from the symbol's *eidetic* meaning,[168] and focused on its *operational*

---

[158] Carnap, *Introduction to Symbolic Logic* ..., p. 2.

[159] WD, p. 10.

[160] On the translation of *Logistik* as symbolic or mathematical logic, see note 63 above.

[161] SZ, p. 159.

[162] Thus Heidegger remarks: "Mit Hilfe von mathematischen Methoden wird versucht, das System der Aussagenverknüpfungen zu errechnen; daher nennt sich diese Logik auch 'mathematische Logik' ". (DF, p. 122.)

[163] As he states in DF: "Was die Logistik beibringt ist nun freilich alles andere, nur keine Logik ...," (DF, p. 122.)

[164] This may be gathered from his statements in DF, for example: "Die Logistik ist vielmehr selbst nur eine auf Sätze und Satzformen angewandte Mathematik." (DF, p. 122.) It is interesting to note that this position of Heidegger's has not changed at all over the years. See for example his first publication, "Neuere Forschungen über Logik," *Literarische Rundschau für das katholische Deutschland*, XXXVIII (1912), col. 570 in which his position on symbolic logic is already clear. For a genetic study of the development of Heidegger's thought on logic from his earliest writings through to his last, see my article, "Heidegger on Logic: A Genetic Study of his Thought on Logic", *Journal of the History of Philosophy*, XII (1974), 77-94.

[165] For a more detailed exposition of the nature of formalism, see for example, Tarski, *Logic, Semantics, Metamathematics* ..., pp. 165-186.

[166] I. Bochenski, *Formale Logik* (München: Freiburg, 1956), p. 311.

[167] US, p. 125.

[168] A sign has eidetic meaning if we know its semantic counterpart, i.e. if we know to what it refers, what it means. Bochenski, *Methods* ..., p. 38.

meaning,[169] that is, how it may be used or operated with — the syntax rules[170] that are applicable to it, and the calculus of connectives. What the sign *means* may not be known, and at this point of the operation at least, is of no interest. How it can be operated with is the sole concern.[171] It is only an operation with signs, a calculation. To use a crude example, it is something like the maneuvering of beads on the abacus, or better perhaps, to use Hermann Weyl's example, like a game of chess where it is determined in advance which moves are allowable and what the relation of each piece to every other piece within the game will be.[172] The whole deduction then proceeds in a strictly formalistic manner, that is, within the context of the proof one may appeal to nothing but the symbols themselves and the formal rules which apply to them.[173] The game is played, so far as this is possible, without human language.[174] According to the celebrated statement of Bertrand Russell, this type of mathematization is a "subject in which we never know what we are talking about, or whether what we are saying is true".[175]

By this, however, we in no way wish to convey the impression that science and logic are a kind of whimsical game. We are, after all, putting rockets on the moon and exploding hydrogen bombs on the basis of their calculations.[176] The goal of formalism *is* knowledge, and it ultimately only fulfills this goal if it is possible to interpret its results eidetically.[177] This is not to say that there are no parts of logistics and the sciences (especially with scientific theories having no model, e.g. quantum theory)[178] which cannot be given an eidetic meaning. Still, in general, it can be said that they lead to consequences which can be interpreted eidetically.

[169] Hermann Weyl, *Philosophy of Mathematics and Natural Science* (Princeton: Princeton Univ. Press, 1949), p. 8.

[170] Understood here as logical syntax, that is, the theory of the mutual relations of symbols, what combinations are allowable. Bochenski, *Formale Logik* ..., p. 311.

[171] Bochenski, *Formale Logik* ..., pp. 325-326.

[172] Hermann Weyl, *The Open World* (New Haven: Yale Univ. Press, 1932), pp. 75-76.

[173] I. Bochenski, *Contemporary European Philosophy* (Berkeley: Univ. of Calif. Press, 1964), pp. 253-254.

[174] As Weyl notes "... the game of deduction proceeds from axioms by rules which take no account of the meaning of formulas. The mathematical game is played in silence, without words ...". "The Mathematical Way of Thinking", *Science*, XCII (1940), p. 438.

[175] Bertrand Russell, *Mysticism and Logic* (London: Allen and Unwin, 1918), p. 75.

[176] DF, p. 11.

[177] Bochenski, *Methods* ..., p. 40.

[178] Heisenberg, *Physics* ..., pp. 178-179.

From this it also follows that it is impossible to *totally* formalize any system.[179] It is true that the rules of system *A* can be formalized in another system, *B*, and that *B* in its turn can be formalized in system *C*, and so to system *N*, but we must stop somewhere and use non-formalized rules. Further, the rules of *A* must already have eidetic meaning for us while *A* is being constructed. This means that in practice formalized systems are nearly always developed by first establishing meaningful signs, then abstracting from their meaning and proceeding to construct the system formalistically, and finally giving an interpretation to the finished system.[180]

Another, and related, problem of language develops for the modern scientist and logician. Because science is not only an individual affair, but much more the work of a community of researchers, the knowledge must be communicated, and the communication must be effected by means of signs, especially the spoken and written word. Accordingly, the discipline of semiotics was developed to answer to this need.[181] Here we cannot enter into a detailed analysis of this highly complex field. What is of importance as far as Heidegger is concerned, however, is that in the need for exact communication a concept of language has emerged in our days which is of decisive importance to modern man, the conception of language as a means of communication.[182] Because of the crucial importance of language, and man's relation to language, for the essence of man itself,[183] the question of language has received increased attention from Heidegger in his later writings. Indeed, the logic problematic itself has been taken up under this larger question of language,[184] as we shall see in some detail in the next chapter.

Now language, as the philosopher of Freiburg understands it, admits of two things. First, it can be reduced to a mere system of signs, available to all, a means of communication.[185] Taken in this way language is like a means of public transportation that everyone rides.[186] This relation to language quickly devitalizes it and it is emptied of its real meaning. It falls under the dominance of the "public" and

---

[179] Bochenski, *Contemporary European Philosophy* ..., p. 260.
[180] Bochenski, *Formale Logik* ..., p. 266.
[181] Bochenski, *Methods* ..., p. 31.
[182] HH, pp. 26-27.
[183] HB, p. 9.
[184] WD, pp. 99-100.
[185] WD, p. 168.
[186] EM, p. 38.

is put to work arranging lines of communication which are universally accessible to all.[187] The original λόγος has been debased to a simple tool or ὄργανον.[188] Second, language can be understood as containing the revelation of Being, as the house of Being.[189] So understood it is certainly no mere tool at man's disposal.[190]

As Heidegger sees it, the modern theories of language which find their expression in the contemporary movement of symbolic logic,[191] while being a legitimate enough enterprise in itself,[192] is in no way to be countenanced when it attempts to set itself up as the only valid approach to language.[193] But since symbolic logic is an outgrowth of *das Mathematische*, which by its very nature always attempts to establish itself as the *sole* judge and supreme rule in the interpretation of Being,[194] it too tends to be dogmatically assertive and tends to set itself up as the sole authority and interpreter of language and logic.[195] Language, for Heidegger, is never adequately understood when viewed only in terms of formalization, or as a communication medium.[196]

Pursuant to the latter end, communications, various information theories have been developed.[197] Within these theories, "ordinary language" is always seen as a kind of failure,[198] that intractable human element that will not submit to formalization. The standard by which language is measured, the goal which it must strive to achieve is formalization.[199] "Natural language", when viewed from this perspective, is always seen negatively as a lack of formalization.[200] This conception of language is an outgrowth of *das Mathematische* which has its roots in the anthropocentric view of the world implicit in Descartes' *ego cogito*.[201] Thus, linguistic analysis, the development of metalinguistics, and symbolic

---

[187] HB, p. 8.

[188] HB, p. 9.

[189] HB, p. 9.

[190] WD, p. 99.

[191] US, p. 160.

[192] On this point he is very clear: "Sie (d.h. Logistik) stellt sich eine mögliche und berechtigte Aufgabe." (DF, p. 122.) My parenthesis. Cf. also US, pp. 160-161.

[193] DF, p. 122.

[194] DF, pp. 78, 80.

[195] US, p. 263.

[196] US, pp. 254, 264; HB, p. 16.

[197] SG, p. 203.

[198] US, p. 264.

[199] US, p. 263.

[200] US, p. 264.

[201] HB, pp. 9-10.

logic[202] are all a part of the more general movement of the metaphysics of the "Will to Will',[203] which has produced modern technology.[204] As Heidegger notes, "metalanguage and the sputnik, metalinguistics and rocket technology are really the same thing".[205] It is the *Ge-Stell*,[206] the drive toward domination, of technicity (*Technik*) which impels it to develop a language which will be pure instrument, that is, formalized language.[207] Formalization is essentially an extension of calculation, which is man's basic posture towards his world. It attempts in its symbolization to absolutely extrude from the symbol all multiplicity of meaning and rigidly fix it in one meaning. Within a formal system the emphasis is on consistency, freedom from internal contradiction,[208] coherence, consequence, and rigor.[209] As Heidegger sees it, the final outcome of this process is the electronic brain and computerization of thought,[210] the kind of "reasoning piano" envisioned by Stanley Jevons.[211] As the great mathematician Henri Poincairé so aptly put it:

> What these *things* are, not only do we not know, but we must not seek to know ... Thus it will be readily understood that, in order to demonstrate a theorem, it is not necessary or even useful to know what it means. We might replace geometry by the *reasoning piano* imagined by Stanley Jevons; or if we prefer, we might imagine a machine where we would put in axioms at one end and take out theorems at the other, like that legendary machine in Chicago where pigs go in alive and come out transformed into hams and sausages.[212]

But all of this is a far cry from language, at least as Heidegger conceives of it. The foundation of language is λόγος[213] which allows Being to emerge into presence, be regathered and held in openness in

---

[202] US, p. 116.

[203] WM, p. 43; US, p. 160; ZS, p. 41.

[204] US, p. 160; HW, pp. 69, 242-246; N, II, pp. 486-487. Cf. also VA, pp. 233-234.

[205] "Metasprache und Sputnik, Metalinguistik und Raketentechnik sind das Selbe." (US, p. 160.)

[206] US, pp. 160, 263.

[207] US, p. 263.

[208] Rudolf Carnap, trans. A. Smeaton, *The Logical Syntax of Language* (London: Routledge and Kegan Paul, 1949), p. 325.

[209] Carnap, *Introduction to Symbolic Logic* ..., pp. 173-174.

[210] SG, p. 203.

[211] "William Stanley Jevons (1835-1882) ... logician and economist; professor of logic and mental and moral philosophy ...". C. I. Lewis, *A Survey of Symbolic Logic* (New York: Dover, 1960), p. 72.

[212] Henri Poincaré, trans. F. Maitland, *Science and Method* (New York: Dover, 1952), p. 152. Poincaré's emphasis.

[213] EM, p. 128.

language. It is in essence mysterious, a revelation that at the same time conceals itself, and hence all attempts to "nail it down", as it were, in words whose meaning is rigidly fixed in univocality must fail.[214] What is crucial for man is to bring language into the truth of Being and to let this penetrate and pervade it.[215] This is crucial for man, for language grounds his historical Dasein, it is his world.[216] If he regards it as the object of his calculations, it will be despoiled as surely as his external world has been laid waste by his drive to dominance expressed in technicity.[217] But language is no mere tool of man, Heidegger insists. It is the house of Being and man's world.[218] What is endangered by man's relating himself to Being and language as objects of his domination and manipulation is nothing less than his own essence.[219] If he is to have an abode appropriate to his essence it is of critical importance that his relation to language be changed from language as a tool, to language as λόγος, rooted in Being as truth.

To conclude then, we might summarize what we have seen as follows. Logic's birth was caused by the forgetfulness of Being as truth, ἀλήθεια.[220] Logic in the sense in which we understand it could only have been born when truth, ἀλήθεια, had been transformed into ἰδέα. When this had happened, it made inevitable a parallel change in λόγος, and thus in Aristotle λόγος is understood as λέγειν τι κατά τινος, to say something of something. This notion of λόγος gave primacy to the proposition, which was the necessary precondition for the development of logic. This new way of understanding λόγος gave rise in the Latin tradition to the notion of *ratio* which, on its own authority, established itself as judge over Being.[221] Classical logic is the precursor of symbolic/ mathematical logic which is another branch of technicity. It has its logical end-point in the electronic brain, where thinking has been reduced to an affair of machines.[222] It is a necessary outgrowth of the mathematical project which had its origin in Descartes' *cogito-sum* in which the world is transformed into a reckonable object of man, now conceived of

[214] N, I, pp. 168-169.
[215] HB, p. 30.
[216] EM, p. 128.
[217] VA, p. 72.
[218] HB, p. 9.
[219] SG, pp. 169-170; HH, pp. 27-28.
[220] EM, pp. 92-93.
[221] EM, p. 147.
[222] WD, p. 145; SG, p. 65.

as subject. The reckoning mind needs an exact instrument, and hence language is formalized. Formalized language, which as part of the mathematizing spirit whose essence it is to establish itself on its own authority as the standard of all knowledge, inherits the characteristics of its parent — it too vaunts itself as *the* authoritative interpretation of language, regarding non-formalized language as a falling off from what is now the standard of perfection in language — formalization. Symbolic logic, as Heidegger sees it, far from being the standard of rigor, consistency, and consequence toward which all logic ought to aim, is merely mathematics applied to propositions which are merely conceptual representation.[223] While a legitimate enough endeavor, it is essentially outside of the realm of logic adequately understood.[224] Logic, as Heidegger understands it, is a reflection on λόγος as it was originally experienced.[225]

Logic, as we now understand the term however, is a far cry from this. It was born of the forgetfulness of Being which took place in the thought of Plato and developed through Aristotle, Descartes and Kant. Kant, as Heidegger interprets him, made a magnificent effort to get out of the mere manipulation of empty concepts and back over to the thing (*das Ding*) through his transcendental logic but his effort must, in the final analysis, be judged a failure. Heidegger reaches this conclusion because as he sees Kant, struggle though he might, he remains imprisoned within the Aristotelian conception of λόγος, that is, to say something of something. Thus, although he struggled valiantly to free himself from the Aristotelian λόγος and the subject-ism of Descartes, the basically mathematical character of Western thought, initiated in the thought of Plato with the changed concept of truth and given a decisive turn in the thought of Descartes, is merely transposed to the transcendental level. The mathematical character of modern thought gains momentum after Descartes especially with Galileo and Newton. As the newly founded physical sciences begin to develop, there is a correlative development in logic. This development manifests itself in an ever increasing drive toward mathematization of logic. This mathematization, in its turn, finds its expression in the increased tendency to absorb all logic into symbolic/mathematical logic. Also, and parallel to this, science places ever increasing demands on logic, which it now

---

[223] DF, p. 122.
[224] DF, p. 122.
[225] DF, p. 122.

regards as its heuristic instrument, for formalization. This latter development, formalization, produces a logic of symbols which, in order to be manipulated with the mathematical precision required by the new sciences, have been emptied of all eidetic meaning. Because of the tremendous success which has been achieved by modern science, the formalized approach of symbolic logic is now judged by nearly all to be the only approach worthy of serious consideration. But while science, using its mathematical instruments, has achieved many outstanding accomplishments, still, these successes have not been without their price. While science has produced wonders in travel in outer space, in the development of electronic brains capable of incredible feats of calculation, in instant communication systems which have turned the world into a "global village", and indeed in nearly every area of our lives, it has also brought with it much that is not so wondrous. The "mathematical" approach to man's world, with its drive toward manipulation, control and exploitation, has also so ravaged this world that the very survival of future generations is now deemed questionable. And while it is true that in the area of architecture, for example, this same "mathematical" spirit of science has been successful in achieving architectural miracles, it is also true that its approach of manipulation and exploitation has spawned violence of an unprecedented ferocity in the cities which it has created. And finally, although one cannot but be in awe at the brilliance of its achievement in unraveling the innermost secrets of the structure of matter, it has thereby also condemned man to live under the Damoclean sword of a nuclear holocaust.

What Heidegger is doing, then, as he reflects on the all-pervasive "mathematical" character of modern thought is tremendously important for contemporary man. He looks at the panorama of the modern world and sees in it many achievements of science greatly to be admired, but he also sees, and realistically it would seem, man living in a world in which his very survival is threatened. The purpose of his reflections on this, and what is important for us, is to seek out the deep, the metaphysical cause of all of this, and thus to change the direction of the flow of Western cultural history.

CHAPTER VI

LOGOS AND LANGUAGE:
THE OVERCOMING OF TECHNICITY

The importance of the present chapter on Being as λόγος to the logic problematic can scarcely be overestimated, because, as Heidegger tells us, since the lecture course of 1934 entitled "Logic," there lies concealed behind this title the transformation of the logic-question into a reflection upon λόγος.

In the summer semester of the year 1934 I gave a lecture course under the title 'Logic.' It was, however, a reflection on λόγος, in which I sought for the essence of language. [1]

Since it is in reflecting on λόγος that Heidegger seeks the essence of logic, an understanding of what he means by λόγος is essential to an understanding of the logic problematic. And further, Heidegger also tells us the logic question was transformed into a quest for the essence of language, which he also seeks in his reflection on λόγος.

Since the lecture course entitled 'Logic' which was held in the summer of 1934, there lies concealed behind this title 'Logic' a "transformation of logic into the quest after the *essence* (*Wesen*) of language ..." [2]

We shall, therefore, attempt now to see what Heidegger understands by λόγος, and how this λόγος is the ground of logic and language, and further, we shall see how, and why, the logic-question should have been transformed into the quest after the essence of language.

In the West thinking has been treated under the rubric "logic." [3] The word logic is derived from the Greek word λόγος. [4] Λόγος, however,

[1] Im Sommersemester des Jahres 1934 hielt ich eine Vorlesung unter dem Titel: 'Logik'. Es war jedoch eine Besinnung auf den λόγος, worin ich das Wesen der Sprache suchte." (US, p. 93.)

[2] "... seit der Vorlesung 'Logik' im Sommer 1934 hinter diesem Titel 'Logik' 'die Verwandlung der Logik in die Frage nach dem *Wesen* der Sprache' verbirgt ..." (WD, p. 100.) Heidegger's emphasis.

[3] Thus Heidegger points out in WD, p. 10: "Das Denken über das Denken hat sich im Abendland als 'Logik' entfaltet."

[4] EM, pp. 91-92.

as experienced in the original dawning of thought did not mean a
doctrine of thought, rules of correct thinking, or even word or discourse.[5]
Λόγος is related to the verb λέγειν — "What λόγος is, we understand
from λέγειν."[6] Λέγειν already at the time of Heraclitus in the sixth century B.C.[7] had the meaning, "to tell," "to relate," "to speak," etc.[8]
There was, however, an even more primordial meaning of the word,[9]
and the later meaning can only be understood on the basis of its more
original meaning of laying and gathering.

... λέγειν in its meaning of 'saying' and 'speaking' can only be understood if
it is considered in the light of its most proper meaning as 'laying' and 'gathering'.[10]

Originally λόγος was experienced as being at one with Being.[11] It was
simply another name for Being — "For ὁ λόγος is the name for
the Being of a being."[12] It is Being in its collectedness.[13] In order
that Being have the possibility of manifesting itself, of emerging into
presence and enduring, it must first be gathered together in unity.

The word ὁ λόγος names that which gathers together every being emerging into
presence into its coming into presence and allows each to lie forth in its presence.
ὁ λόγος names that by which the emergence into presence of the presencing
comes to pass. The emergence into presence of the presencing is called by
the Greeks τὸ ἐόν, i.e. ... the Being of a being.[14]

Λόγος therefore, originally had the sense of gathered togetherness —
"The λόγος is the original gathered togetherness of the original gathering ..."[15] It is this gatheredness which makes possible the revelation
of Being as truth.[16]

---

[5] EM, p. 142.

[6] "Was λόγος ist, entnehmen wir dem λέγειν." (VA, p. 208.)

[7] EM, p. 98.

[8] VA, pp. 208, 228.

[9] VA, p. 208. Cf. also WD, p. 121; EM, pp. 95, 98-99.

[10] "... das λέγειν in seiner Bedeutung von 'sagen' und 'reden' nur verstehbar ist wenn
es in eigenster Bedeutung als 'legen' und 'lesen' bedacht wird." (VA, p. 223.)

[11] VA, p. 227.

[12] "Denn ὁ λόγος ist der Name für das Sein des Seienden." (VA, p. 228.)

[13] EM, p. 100.

[14] "Das Wort ὁ λόγος nennt jenes, das alles Anwesende ins Anwesen versammelt
und darin vorliegen lässt. Ὁ λόγος nennt jenes, worin sich das Anwesen des Anwesenden
ereignet. Das Anwesen des Anwesenden heisst bei den Griechen τὸ ἐόν, d.h. ... das Sein
des Seienden." (VA, p. 227.)

[15] "Der λόγος ist die ursprüngliche Versammlung der anfänglichen Lese ..." (VA,
pp. 215-216.)

[16] VA, p. 213. Cf. also EM, p. 130.

Insofar as the λόγος allows that which lies forth to lie forth as such it discloses that which is presencing itself in its emergence into presence. This disclosure is ἀλήθεια. 'Αλήθεια and λόγος are the same. The λέγειν allows ἀλήθεια, that which is disclosed as such to lie forth.[17]

Λόγος is also, therefore, the opposite of concealment.[18]

Originally λέγειν meant to collect, to gather, especially in the sense of a harvesting as with grapes or wheat.[19] That it could also come to mean "to make manifest," "to allow to appear," can only be understood if its essential relation to φύσις is borne in mind. The power which emerges from concealment must be gathered together, one. "To gather together here stands in opposition to concealment. To gather together is here to re-veal, to make manifest."[20] Thus λέγειν also had the sense of δηλοῦν,[21] "to make manifest," which was retained even in Plato, as well as ἀποφαίνεσθαι, to-bring-to-show-itself, which can still be seen in Aristotle.

Thus the λόγος has the character of δηλοῦν, making manifest, not only in Heraclitus, but also in Plato. Aristotle characterizes the λέγειν of the λόγος as ἀποφαίνεσθαι, to bring to self-manifestation.[22]

The apophantic character of λέγειν can also be seen underlying its meaning, "to lay."[23] "To lay" is to allow something to lie before us.[24] When we say something,[25] when we recount an event,[26] when we "lay a request before someone" we make it lie forth in openness before us.[27] The very essence, then, of λέγειν and λόγος for the Greeks may

---

[17] "Insofern der λόγος das Vorliegende als ein solches vorliegen lässt, entbirgt er das Anwesende in sein Anwesen. Das Entbergen aber ist die ἀλήθεια. Diese und der λόγος sind das Selbe. Das λέγειν lässt ἀλήθεια, Unverborgenes als solches vorliegen." (VA, p. 220.)

[18] EM, p. 130.

[19] P, in *Wegmarken*, p. 348; VA, p. 209; WD, p. 125.

[20] "Sammeln steht hier im Gegensatz zum Verbergen. Sammeln ist hier ent-bergen, offenbar machen." (EM, p. 130.) Cf. also EM, pp. 94, 95, 96, 103-104.

[21] SZ, p. 32.

[22] "So hat der λόγος nicht nur bei *Heraklit*, sondern noch bei *Platon* den Charakter des δηλοῦν, des Offenbarmachens. *Aristoteles* kennzeichnet das λέγειν des λόγος als ἀποφαίνεσθαι zum-sich-zeigen-bringen ..." (EM, p. 130.) Cf. also SZ, p. 32; VA, p. 213.

[23] SZ, pp. 32-33, 219-220. Cf. also Ernst Tugendhat, *Der Wahrheitsbegriff bei Husserl und Heidegger* ..., pp. 333-334.

[24] WD, p. 123.

[25] VA, p. 212. Cf. also WD, pp. 122, 123.

[26] WD, p. 121.

[27] WD, p. 123; SZ, pp. 32-33.

be gathered from these several related meanings. It is a laying in the sense that it allows that which is collected and gathered into one to lie forth in openness before us.²⁸ Λόγος is itself the result of λέγειν as gathering and collecting,²⁹ and therefore is collectedness into unity.³⁰ Λόγος is another name for Being.³¹ It is the intrinsic power of Being to lie forth in a gathered unity. It is indissolubly bound to both φύσις and ἀλήθεια.

Φύσις and λόγος are the same. ἀλήθεια and λόγος are the same ...³²

Before Being can emerge from concealment, come to presence, appear and abide (φύσις-ἀλήθεια) it must be gathered into unity (λόγος). But since Being, Dasein, and νοεῖν are not experienced initially in an isolated separation from each other,³³ λόγος is essentially related to Dasein. If Being's appearance is not to be nugatory, there must be a λόγος corresponding to its λόγος; it needs something to gather it in, an "homologous" structure as it were, that is to say there must be a ὁμολογεῖν.

... the λόγος stands in need of the ὁμολογεῖν if that which is presencing is to shine forth and appear.³⁴

Man in an essential sense is attuned to the silent voice of Being.³⁵ If he speaks it is only because he has first of all been spoken to. "... Authentically language speaks, not man. Man speaks only insofar as he at all times re-sponds to language."³⁶ If he speaks, it is because he has first heard and heeded the voice of Being. Here we must understand hearing (Hören) as an attentive listening (Horchsamkeit),³⁷ a harkening, an essential attunement. Fundamentally, hearing (Hören) is Dasein's belonging to (gehören) Being,³⁸ its obedience (Gehorsam)³⁹

²⁸ VA, p. 211.
²⁹ VA, p. 215.
³⁰ VA, p. 215.
³¹ VA, p. 229; EM, pp. 101-102; US, pp. 185, 237.
³² "Φύσις und λόγος sind dasselbe." (EM, p. 100.) "ἀλήθεια ... und der λόγος sind das Selbe ..." (VA, p. 220.)
³³ WD, pp. 126-127.
³⁴ "... der λόγος das ὁμολογεῖν braucht, wenn Anwesendes im Anwesen scheinen und erscheinen soll." (VA, p. 226.)
³⁵ WM, p. 50.
³⁶ "... eigentlich spricht die Sprache, nicht der Mensch. Der Mensch spricht erst, insofern er jeweils der Sprache entspricht." (HH, p. 26.)
³⁷ VA, p. 214.
³⁸ VA, p. 216.
³⁹ VA, p. 214.

to the call of Being. If the λέγειν is a laying which allows that which is spoken to lie forth in its gathered and gathering unity,[40] a cor-responding λέγειν (ὁμολογεῖν) of Dasein is required so that that which has been laid forth in openness may lie forth in the unified collectedness of its oneness.[41] In this way λόγος, as a gathered gathering which lets lie forth in openness that which has been collected into a unity, is brought to pass.[42] But the λόγος which is the very definition of man must be clearly distinguished from the λόγος which is another name for Being.

Authentic hearing belongs to the λόγος. Therefore this hearing itself is a λέγειν. Authentic hearing of mortals, as such, is, in a certain manner, the same as the λόγος. Nevertheless precisely as ὁμολογεῖν it is by no means the same. It is not the λόγος itself.[43]

The λόγος which Dasein is, is a ὁμολογεῖν, that is, it is an attentive and obedient attunement to the voice of Being. But this requires, at least in terms of ontological priority, that Being has revealed itself through a λέγειν which has issued in Being as λόγος: that which is re-gathered in the ὁμολογεῖν presupposes that it previously lie forth in openness in a collected oneness.[44]

From the consideration of λόγος in its relation to ὁμολογεῖν we see too how man could be defined by the Greeks as ζῷον λόγον ἔχον, not in the later decadent sense in which the λόγος is merely an externalized "faculty"[45] or "power of reason"[46] which sets itself up as judge over Being,[47] but rather in the sense that to be human means to take gathering upon oneself (λόγος).[48] Being as overpowering appearing requires a cor-responding λόγος. It is λόγος in this sense that pervades and grounds human-being.[49] Being human *is* λόγος, the gathering,[50]

---

[40] VA, p. 215.

[41] VA, p. 215.

[42] VA, p. 215.

[43] "Das eigentliche Hören gehört dem λόγος. Deshalb ist dieses Hören selbst ein λέγειν. Als solches ist das eigentliche Hören der Sterblichen in gewisser Weise das Selbe wie der λόγος. Gleichwohl ist es gerade als ὁμολογεῖν ganz und gar nicht das Selbe. Es ist nicht selber der λόγος selbst." (VA, p. 217.)

[44] VA, p. 217.

[45] EM, pp. 108, 134.

[46] EM, p. 134.

[47] EM, p. 136.

[48] EM, p. 133.

[49] EM, p. 134.

[50] EM, p. 129.

the bringing to manifestation of the overpowering eruption into presence of Being.

Being-human is, according to its historical, history disclosing essence, *Logos*, gathering and apperception of the Being of being: the happening of that strangest being, in which, through violence, the overpowering comes into appearance and is brought to a stand.[51]

We are now in a position to see how λόγος could be so closely related to language, and indeed be the very ground of language.[52] As Being reveals itself to Dasein it is gathered in, harvested, and collected. "Man is, as the one who stands in Logos, in the gathering, active — he is the gatherer."[53] This gathering comes about in thought which is a vital union of Dasein and Being. Fecundated by Being,[54] thought then expresses Being in the word,[55] λόγος, which is a gathering of Being which holds Being open in its disclosure.[56]

The word, naming, re-gathers the being which is opening itself from out of its surge into Being, and preserves it in this openness ... In original saying the Being of a being is opened up in the structure of its gatheredness.[57]

Λόγος is a primordial happening (*Geschehen*) or coming to pass of unconcealment of truth, ἀλήθεια — "Logos as gathering is originally a happening of unconcealment."[58] Naming therefore is the most primordial act of Dasein,[59] since thought itself is in the service of language (*Sprache*). It is in naming that Being first comes into openness in

---

[51] "Das Menschsein ist nach seinem geschichtlichen, Geschichte eröffnenden Wesen *Logos*, Sammlung und Vernehmung des Seins des Seienden: das Geschehnis jenes Unheimlichsten, in dem durch die Gewalt-tätigkeit das Überwältigende zur Erscheinung kommt und zum Stand gebracht wird." (EM, p. 131.)

[52] EM, pp. 130-132; WD, p. 171.

[53] "Der Mensch ist als der im Logos, in der Sammlung, Stehende und Tätige: der Sammler." (EM, pp. 131-132.)

[54] WD, p. 139.

[55] VA, p. 223; HD, p. 38.

[56] This point is made by Buddeberg: "Immer will mit dem Wort etwas offenbar gemacht, etwas sehen, etwas erkennen gelassen werden. Das Wort als logos hat also von vornherein einen ausgezeichneten Bezug zur Wahrheit." (*Heidegger und die Dichtung* ..., p. 5.)

[57] "Das Wort, das Nennen stellt das sich eröffnende Seiende aus dem unmittelbaren überwältigenden Andrang in sein Sein zurück und bewahrt es in dieser Offenheit ... Im ursprünglichen Sagen wird das Sein des Seienden im Gefüge seiner Gesammeltheit eröffnet." (EM, p. 131.)

[58] "Anfänglich *ist* der Logos als Sammlung das Geschehen der Unverborgenheit ..." (EM, p. 142.)

[59] DF, p. 19.

the word.[60] The act of naming clothes Being in a word.[61] Language is the house of Being.[62] It is in this house that man lives.[63] Man *lives* in language.[64] It is the result of a constant dialogue (*Ent-sprechen*)[65] between Dasein and Being.[66] Far from being simply a handy tool to be plied according to Dasein's good pleasure, or merely a *means* of communication,[67] it is the very life-giving and life-sustaining environment in which Dasein has its being, which makes it possible for Dasein to stand in openness.

Language is not merely a tool which man also possesses among many others, but rather that which first makes it possible for him to stand in the openness of being.[68]

In order to show as forcefully as possible that language is not simply something at Dasein's disposal, a tool to be utilized as others which are available, Heidegger employs the enigmatic expression which occurs so frequently in *Unterwegs zur Sprache*, "die Sprache spricht ..."[69] It is language that speaks, not man. What are we to make of this puzzling statement? As is the case with many such startling statements of Heidegger,[70] they can only be properly understood if they are seen in the light of their polemical character.[71] The all too prevalent tendency today is to view language simply as a tool, or a means of communication.

In the present age, as a consequence of the haste of commonplaceness of daily speech and writing, another relationship to language comes ever more decisively into predominance. We mean namely, that language also, as all other things

[60] EM, p. 11; HB, p. 54; HW, pp. 60-61; US, pp. 30, 237; See also Buddeberg, *Heidegger und die Dichtung ...*, p. 32.

[61] WD, p. 85.

[62] HB, pp. 21-22.

[63] HB, pp. 5, 9, 45; US, pp. 166, 267.

[64] VA, p. 228.

[65] WP, p. 44; HH, p. 26.

[66] ID, p. 22; WP, pp. 35-36.

[67] EM, p. 38; HB, pp. 8, 58, 59, 60; HW, p. 60; HH, pp. 26-27.

[68] "Die Sprache ist nicht nur ein Werkzeug, das der Mensch neben vielen anderen auch besitzt, sondern sie gewährt überhaupt erst die Möglichkeit, inmitten der Offenheit von Seiendem zu stehen." (HD, p. 35.)

[69] Cf. for example, US, pp. 12, 13, 14, 16, 19, 20, 28, 30, 32, 33, 254, 255, 262, 263, 265; also WD, p. 87; HH, p. 34.

[70] For example, "... die Wissenschaft ihrerseits nicht denkt und nicht denken kann ..." (WD, p. 4); "... der Mensch allein existiert ..." (WM, p. 15); "... das Wesen der Wahrheit ist die Un-wahrheit ..." (HW, p. 43).

[71] On this point see for example, Marx, "Heidegger's New Concept ...," p. 456; Heinemann, *Existenzphilosophie ...*, p. 95.

of daily routine with which we deal, is an instrument of communication and information. This representation of language is so common to us that we hardly note its uncanny power.[72]

In Heidegger's view this notion of language represents an almost unbelievable debasement of the true character of language.[73] Latent in the statement, "die Sprache spricht ...", is a question of crucial importance. Heidegger's purpose here is to change completely the relationship between man and language from one in which man *uses* language, to one in which he *serves* it. This can be clearly seen from the following passage:

> This cor-responding is a speech. It stands in service to *language*. It is difficult for us to understand today what this means, since our customary representation of language has undergone a strange transformation. As a consequence of this, language appears as an instrument of expression. Accordingly, people take it as correct to say: language is in the service of thought, instead of: thought as cor-respondence is in the service of language.[74]

It is precisely the present relationship of *usage* which brings about the commonplaceness in language, and which ultimately must issue in its death.

> To speak language is something completely different from using a language. Customary speech only uses language. Its commonplaceness consists precisely in this relationship to language.[75]

Viewing language as an instrument has resulted in emptying it of its richness, its flexibility, its mystery,[76] and freezing words into the rigidity of univocal meanings. But the word has, rather, manifold meanings

---

[72] "Im gegenwärtigen Zeitalter bringt sich aber zufolge der Hast und Gewöhnlichkeit des alltäglichen Redens und Schreibens ein anderes Verhältnis zur Sprache immer entschiedener in die Vorherrschaft. Wir meinen nämlich auch die Sprache sei nur, wie alles Tägliche sonst, womit wir umgehen, ein Instrument, und zwar das Instrument der Verständigung und der Information. Diese Vorstellung von der Sprache ist uns so geläufig, dass wir ihre unheimliche Macht kaum bemerken." (HH, pp. 26-27.)

[73] US, p. 15.

[74] "Dieses Ent-sprechen ist ein Sprechen. Es steht im Dienst der *Sprache*. Was dies heisst, ist für uns heute schwer zu verstehen; denn unsere geläufige Vorstellung von der Sprache hat seltsame Wandlungen durchgemacht. Ihnen zufolge erscheint die Sprache als ein Instrument des Ausdrucks. Demgemäss hält man es für richtiger zu sagen: die Sprache steht im Dienst des Denkens, statt: das Denken als Ent-sprechen steht im Dienst der Sprache." (WP, p. 44.)

[75] "Die Sprache sprechen ist etwas völlig anderes als eine Sprache benützen. Das gewöhnliche Sprechen benützt nur die Sprache. Seine Gewöhnlichkeit besteht gerade in diesem Verhältnis zur Sprache." (WD, p. 87.)

[76] WD, pp. 168-169.

and nuances corresponding to the mystery of Being which it expresses.[77] When the word is reduced to the rigidity of a univocal meaning, which is the necessary pre-condition for the development of the formalization of language,[78] the electronic brain, and language machines[79] (all of which in Heidegger's view are related phenomena), language, which can only express the mysteriousness of Being in words which are highly flexible and manifold in meaning, has been killed with the same stroke.

The life of genuine language consists in the manifoldness of meanings. The transformation of the living, constantly varying words, into the rigidity of a univocal mechanically established system of signs would be the death of language, and the freezing and desolation of Dasein.[80]

This also destroys man's world — "nur wo Sprache, da ist Welt."[81] Thus, behind the seeming nonsense statement, "die Sprache spricht ...", there is a purpose of crucial importance — to change completely the relationship of man to language. What is involved in the language question, as Heidegger views the matter, is no less than a threat to man himself.[82] It is the very essence of man, whose essence is formed by his relation to language and sustained by it, which is at stake.[83]

---

[77] Concerning the notion of mystery (*Geheimnis*) as the origin of language and the relation of the word to mystery Buddeberg notes the following in her interpretation of Heidegger: "Dem Denker scheint die Sprache aus demselben Grund des Geheimnisses aufzusteigen, in dem sie auch für den Dichter ruhte; dieses Geheimnis, in das Hölderlin selbst so tief eingelassen war. In seiner Erscheinung ist wohl auf eine einmalige Weise das ursprüngliche Wahrheitswalten im Wesen des Wortes offenbar geworden." (*Heidegger und die Dichtung* ..., p. 16.)

[78] US, pp. 263-264.

[79] HH, p. 27; US, pp. 160-161.

[80] "Das Wesen der wirklichen Sprache besteht in der Vieldeutigkeit. Die Umschaltung des lebendigen, schwingenden Wortes in die Starrheit einer eindeutig, mechanisch festgelegten Zeichenfolge wäre der Tod der Sprache und die Vereisung und Verödung des Daseins." (N, I, pp. 168-169.)

[81] HD, p. 35.

[82] SG, pp. 169-170; HH, pp. 27-28.

[83] Thus Heidegger remarks in one of his last published statements entitled *Zeichen* which deals with the technicizing (*Technisierung*) of language and the threat that this poses to man: "Die Sprache, als blosse Zeichengebung vorgestellt, bietet den Ansatz für die informationstheoretische Technisierung der Sprache. Die von hier aus einsetzende Einrichtung des Verhältnisses des Menschen zur Sprache vollzieht auf die umheimlichste Weise die Forderung von Karl Marx: 'Es gilt die Welt zu verändern.' Ob man die radikale Unmenschlichkeit der jetzt bestaunten Wissenschaft einmal einsieht und noch rechtzeitig zugibt? Die Übermacht des rechnenden Denkens schlägt täglich entschiedener auf den Menschen selbst zurück und entwürdigt ihn zum bestellbaren Bestandstück eines masslosen 'operationalen' Modelldenkens." (*Neue Zürcher Zeitung*, Nr. 579, p. 51.)

"Language is the clearing and concealing advent of Being itself",[84] not a tool[85] which man disposes of according to the whim of the moment. Thought is called into the service of Being in order to bring the truth of Being into disclosure through language.[86] Through authentic thought, Dasein and Being work together on the building of the house of Being which is language, λόγος.[87] Λόγος, then, is the essential foundation of language — "The Logos gives the ground of the essence of language."[88] There can be true speech only so long as it is directed toward and founded upon Being as λόγος.[89] Human speech is not a power that man has among others, such as laughter or the ability to use tools.[90] It is that which makes human-being to be *human*-being.

The theory is true that the distinction between man and plants and animals is based upon his ability to speak. The statement means not only that man possesses among other faculties also the power of speech. The statement means, rather, only language enables man to be that sort of a living being that he as man is. Only as a speaking being is man man.[91]

Neither human-being, nor human speech are adequately grasped when they are viewed from the perspective of a nature which man has in common with the other animals.[92] Further, and this is of the greatest importance to the logic problematic, language is never adequately represented when seen only in its symbolic character.[93] The essence of the calculus which is applied to propositions in symbolic logic, which finally issues in "thought-machines" and electronic brains, is based upon the univocal meaning of words.[94] But the formalization of language, the freezing into univocality of meaning, which is a necessary condition

[84] "Sprache ist lichtend-verbergende Ankunft des Seins selbst." (HB, p. 16.)

[85] "Die Sprache ist aber kein Werkzeug." (WD, p. 99.)

[86] HB, pp. 5, 30; WM, p. 50.

[87] HB, p. 24.

[88] Der Logos begründet das Wesen der Sprache." (EM, p. 128.)

[89] EM, p. 101.

[90] P, in *Wegmarken*, p. 348.

[91] "Die Lehre gilt, der Mensch sei im Unterschied zu Pflanze und Tier das sprachfähige Lebewesen. Der Satz meint nicht nur, der Mensch besitze neben anderen Fähigkeiten auch diejenige zu sprechen. Der Satz will sagen, erst die Sprache befähige den Menschen, dasjenige Lebewesen zu sein, das er als Mensch ist. Als der Sprechende ist der Mensch: Mensch." (US, p. 11.)

[92] HB, p. 16.

[93] WD, p. 168; HB, p. 16.

[94] On this point see for example, A. F. Lingis, "On the Essence of Technique," *Heidegger and the Quest for Truth* ..., pp. 126-127; Paul Ricœur, *History and Truth*, trans. Charles Kelbley (Evanston: Northwestern Univ. Press, 1965), p. 202.

for the development of symbolic logic, as we noted in the last chapter, is the very death of language.[95] From this it can be seen why the logic problematic since the logic lectures of 1934 had been transformed into the question of the essential nature of language, and its treatment subsumed under this larger question,[96] as we noted at the beginning of this chapter.

Therefore Heidegger, in taking up the question of symbolic logic in the middle thirties in a lecture course entitled "Questions Concerning the Ground of Metaphysics" (1935-36), which was published in 1962 as DF, is concerned to show that while it is a valid and worthwhile enterprise, it does not reach the ultimate foundations of logic.

The characterization of the assertion as the connection of representations is correct but unsatisfying.. This correct, but inadequate, definition of the assertion became the basis for a conception and treatment of logic which is much discussed today, and has been much talked about for a number of decades; this type of logic is called symbolic logic (*Logistik*). With the help of mathematical methods it attempts to calculate the system of connectives between assertions. Therefore this logic is also called 'mathematical logic'. It proposes for itself a possible and justified task. What symbolic logic achieves, however, is something quite different from logic, provided we understand logic as a reflection upon the λόγος.[97]

In this text and in the section immediately preceding it Heidegger states clearly and explicitly that the interpretation of the proposition which was developed in traditional logic is not "incorrect;" there is no question of Heidegger interpreting traditional logic as one large mistake that reaches back to Plato and Aristotle, which he will now at this late date in history correct. Rather, he says repeatedly that the treatment of the proposition in traditional logic is correct, but it is also inadequate. And so with symbolic logic — its work is valuable and certainly justifiable, Heidegger concedes, but as with traditional logic, it is not an adequate approach if one wishes to get to the problem of the ultimate grounding of either traditional logic or symbolic logic.

---

[95] N, I, pp. 168-169.

[96] WD, pp. 99-100. Cf. also US, p. 93.

[97] "Die Kennzeichnung der Aussage als Vorstellungsverknüpfung ist richtig, aber unbefriedigend. Diese richtige, aber unzureichende Aussagedefinition ist die Grundlage für eine Auffassung und Bearbeitung der Logik geworden, die heute und seit einigen Jahrzehnten viel von sich reden macht und Logistik genannt wird. Mit Hilfe von mathematischen Methoden wird versucht, das System der Aussageverknüpfungen zu errechnen; daher nennt sich diese Logik auch 'mathematische Logik'. Sie stellt sich eine mögliche und berechtigte Aufgabe. Was die Logistik beibringt, ist nun freilich alles andere, nur keine Logik, d.h. eine Besinnung auf den λόγος." (DF, p. 122.)

The text here from 1935-36 says, in effect practically the same thing as the report of 1912, *Neuere Forschungen über Logik*.⁹⁸ Symbolic logic still raises the same foundational problem in 1935-36 as it did in 1912. And so the problem of foundation will continue to be insoluble so long as the approach does not seek a more ultimate grounding than is given within symbolic logic itself. This foundation, as Heidegger sees it, can only be laid bare through a more primordial grasp of λόγος than is experienced in logic. Before there can be a logic (in the sense of traditional logic or symbolic logic) Being must have the possibility of revealing itself. Λόγος is the power by which Being as gathered together unity ("Εν-Πάντα) can lie forth in openness. Without the openness of Being which λόγος makes possible there could be no logic at all. If one is seeking for an ultimate ground of logic, then one must seek an approach which moves on a different level than the approach which has been taken by either the traditional Aristotelian logic, or the contemporary approach of symbolic logic. Foundational questions require a thinking which is also foundational. Therefore Heidegger speaks about a logic which reflects upon λόγος (*Besinnung auf den* λόγος)⁹⁹ as experienced by the early Greeks, that is, λογος as gathered unity which makes possible the manifestation of Being as truth. The λόγος which Heidegger sought as he moved more and more deeply into the Being-question could not be the λόγος of traditional logic, that is, the proposition which asserts something about something already present. What was required, rather, was a comprehension of λογος which would cor-respond to Being, but not Being as present-ness of what is already present, but Being as truth, ἀλήθεια, revealing-concealment.

In this movement of Heidegger's thought the logic-question came to be transformed into the question which is, for Heidegger, more primordial, the question of language, and the relation of language to Being. By 1934 this transformation had already occurred.

Since the lecture course entitled "Logic" which was held in the summer of 1934, there lies concealed behind this title "Logic" a transformation of logic into the quest after the essence (Wesen) of language ..."¹⁰⁰

⁹⁸ NF, cols. 465-472, 517-524, 567-570.

⁹⁹ DF, p. 122; US, p. 93.

¹⁰⁰ "... seit der Vorlesung 'Logik' im Sommer 1934 hinter diesem Titel 'Logik' 'die Verwandlung der Logik in die Frage nach dem *Wesen* der Sprache' verbirgt ..." (WD, p. 100.)

The logic-question is now seen from the deeper perspective of language, and so it is approached as a reflection on λόγος as the foundation of language.

In the summer semester of the year 1934 I gave a lecture course under the title 'Logik'. It was, however, a reflection on λόγος, in which I sought for the essence of language.[101]

From this it becomes clear why Heidegger in treating of symbolic logic in the course entitled "Questions Concerning the Ground of Metaphysics," which took place the following year should say that the approach to the question of the ground of language, if it is to be dealt with adequately must now be seen from the standpoint of a reflection on λόγος. By the time of the Heraclitus interpretation which is presented in the essay Λόγος,[102] published in 1951, which is the distillation of a lecture course of 1944 entitled "Logic,"[103] the union between λόγος as essence(-ing) (Wesen, verbal) of language and Being has been so successfully established that λόγος and Being are seen as inseparably bound together; λόγος is in fact another name for Being. Being as gathered unity lying forth in openness.

As the logic-question becomes transformed into the language-question in the middle 1930's, that is to say about the time of the celebrated *Kehre*, or "turn" in Heidegger's way,[104] the treatment of logic and in particular of symbolic logic also changes. In SZ Heidegger was attempting to lay the foundation of ontology and hence he could view his work as foundational ontology which would overcome the forgetfulness of Being which had characterized Western metaphysics, and think through to the forgotten ground of metaphysics, the sense of Being as truth.

In the Kant book of 1929 Heidegger could still see a similarity between his task and Kant's, that is, establishing the foundation of

---

[101] "Im Sommersemester des Jahres 1934 hielt ich eine Vorlesung unter dem Titel, 'Logik'. Es war jedoch eine Besinnung auf den λόγος, worin ich das Wesen der Sprache suchte." (US, p. 93.)

[102] VA, pp. 207-229.

[103] VA, p. 284.

[104] Concerning the dating of the "turn" see especially Richardson, *Through Phenomenology* ..., pp. 243-245. For Richardson, the "turn" manifests itself in WW (1930). The same work is also seen as the turning point by Tugendhat, *Der Wahrheitsbegriff* ..., pp. 377-387. This placing of the *Kehre* is confirmed by Heidegger himself in an interview published in *L'Express*: Question: "Et votre nouveau style d'interrogation, disons poétique, après 'Être et Temps'?" Heidegger: "Ce n'est qu'un tournant. Ma conférence sur 'L'Essence de la vérité' en est, en quelque sorte, la charnière." (*Express* ..., p. 84.)

ontology.[105] After 1929, however, even the term ontology is dropped, at least as it would apply to his own work, since it too readily lends itself to the misunderstanding that Heidegger's work will remain within the same general framework of the traditional metaphysics.[106] In a work dating from the middle 'thirties which represents the distillation of his thought between the years 1936 to 1946[107] which bears the title *The Overcoming of Metaphysics*,[108] Heidegger no longer speaks of the destruction (*Destruktion*) of the history of ontology as he had in SZ[109] but of its "overcoming" (*Überwindung*), which he understands to be a returning to the forgotten ground of metaphysics.[110] Metaphysics, characterized by the subject versus object stance, is seen as playing the decisive role in the development of the catastrophic conditions of the modern world which threaten the extinction of man himself.[111] The seed that was planted at the time of Plato when truth became something to be looked at, and which developed in the Cartesian subject-object split[112] reached its consummation in Nietzsche[113] in *Übermensch* and *der Wille zur Macht*.[114] Man addresses himself to his world in terms of an aggressive assault which has transformed his world into a wasteland, and in which man himself, conceived by metaphysics as an animal who works, becomes the victim of his own devices.[115] The technicity which is the indispensable tool in these developments is seen as the most significant, and perhaps final moment of metaphysics.[116]

But what has all of this to do with the logic-question? As noted above, with the "turn" in Heidegger's way, there is also a change in the statements about logic and symbolic logic in particular. In the earlier period of his work, Heidegger, as we have seen, was concerned with the problems of foundation that had been raised by the new developments

[105] KM, p. 13. See also Richardson, "Kant and the Late Heidegger ...," p. 126; Koza, *Das Problem des Grundes in Heideggers Auseinandersetzung mit Kant* ..., pp. 7-14.
[106] WM, p. 21. Cf. also HB, pp. 41-42.
[107] VA, p. 283.
[108] "Überwindung der Metaphysik," VA, pp. 71-99.
[109] SZ, pp. 19-27.
[110] VA, p. 71. Cf. also WM, pp. 9-11; and Pöggeler, *Der Denkweg* ..., pp. 143-144.
[111] VA, pp. 72-73, 80, 98-99.
[112] VA, pp. 74, 84-85.
[113] VA, pp. 79, 83.
[114] VA, pp. 79, 82-83.
[115] VA, pp. 72-73, 98-99.
[116] VA, pp. 80, 99; US, p. 116.

in symbolic logic. As we move into the late 'thirties and beyond, symbolic logic is seen more and more as an extremely significant manifestation of metaphysics, and more precisely to be another, and extremely important, manifestation of the spirit of technicity.[117] In the *Overcoming of Metaphysics* it is regarded as another face of metaphysics.[118] It is seen by Heidegger as part of man's calculative posture toward his world which is so characteristic of metaphysics,[119] and as an indispensable tool for the advancement of technicity. By 1952, in the last series of lectures given at Freiburg before his retirement Heidegger remarks:

At the present time in many places, particularly in the Anglo-Saxon countries, symbolic logic is already held to be the only possible form of rigorous philosophy because its results and procedures yield something which is of immediate and certain utility for the building of the technological world.[120]

It is seen as playing a vitally important role in the planetarian technicizing (*Technisierung*) of man.[121]

Why should symbolic logic's role be given such importance? If we recall that the logic-question is seen in terms of the more fundamental question of language, and further that language is viewed as the abode in which man dwells, the only habitation in which he can abide as man, then it becomes clear that a threat to language is a threat to man himself. Heidegger sees in the increasing emphasis which is placed upon the formalization of language something which is symptomatic of man's estate in the modern world. As Heidegger sees it, to approach the essence of language from the standpoint of symbolic logic, to locate the essence of language in an ideal symbolic language, and to view language as spoken by men in the world as a falling off from a symbolic ideal,[122] is not only to endanger language, but by the same stroke to endanger man himself.[123] To destroy man's language is to destroy the only element

---

[117] VA, p. 234.

[118] VA, p. 76.

[119] WD, p. 10.

[120] "Die Logistik gilt jetzt vielerorts, vor allem in den angelsächsischen Ländern, schon als die einzig mögliche Gestalt der strengen Philosophie, weil ihre Ergebnisse und ihr Verfahren sogleich einen sicheren Nutzen für den Bau der technischen Welt abwerfen." (WD, p. 10.)

[121] WD, p. 102.

[122] US, pp. 263-264.

[123] N, I, p. 169.

in which he can live as man.[124] Therefore to destroy this element without which he cannot exist as man, is, in effect to destroy man.

Under the impact of technicity language is viewed merely as an instrument, just as the beings of man's world are seen only as available commodities to be manipulated and ruthlessly exploited according to the whim which rules at the moment.[125] Since symbolic logic has been found to be a useful instrument in the communications media,[126] and in the advancement of technology this approach to language has been so emphasized that all other approaches to it are either excluded or totally ignored.[127]

It is this view of language that Heidegger wishes to combat. As Heidegger views the matter language is only adequately understood when seen in its relationship to λόγος and grounded in it. Two questions may now be raised. Why does he wish to conceive of language in this way, and what is the value of his contribution to a philosophy of language? As we have noted, the logic-question has been transformed into the language-question, and this language-question has become the central preoccupation of the late Heidegger. The reason why the language-question has assumed this importance in the later writings of Heidegger is clear — he views the problem of language as part of a larger issue, that of technicity. The spirit of technicity is itself the result of a basic disorientation of man toward Being. The Faustian stance of man toward Being in which he views Being and beings as things to be controlled and manipulated for his advantage has caused such diverse phenomena as the despoliation of the earth, the age of atomic bombs, the standardization of man, and in terms of language, mass communications media, thought machines and electronic brains. All of these phenomena have conspired to produce an environment in which man cannot live as *man*. For this reason Heidegger wishes to attack what he views as the root cause of all of this, rather than merely treating symptoms. As he sees it, this root cause is man's relation to Being. It is for this reason that Western metaphysics must be "overcome," since its basic position has been to re-present (*vor-stellen*) Being as a being. The re-presentative thought which characterizes metaphysics has produced technicity with its posture of control and manipulation of beings.

[124] US, p. 266.
[125] US, p. 263; HH, pp. 26-27; "Zeichen", *Neue Zürcher Zeitung* ..., p. 51.
[126] SG, p. 203.
[127] HH, pp. 26-27.

But how is Western metaphysics and its characteristic mode of thought (*das vor-stellende Denken*) to be overcome? It will be overcome through the work of the thinker and the poet, since for both, thinking is not the re-presenting (*vor-stellen*) of beings, but rather a receptive attunement to Being. For Heidegger this has meant emphasizing the role of the poet, since the poet, by the very nature of the case, is not a controller and manipulator of Being or beings, but rather one who has received Being's revelation and clothed it in words. Thus, in effect, Western metaphysics will have been overcome when man dwells poetically. This is simply to say that when man dwells poetically a change in his relation to Being will have taken place.[128]

From this it can be seen that the basic thrust of Heidegger's thought concerning language is a humanistic one, although not a humanism in the sense of a new philosophical anthropology, a designation which he has steadfastly rejected as simply treating surface phenomena. What Heidegger is attempting is a radical transformation in man's relation to Being, since it is the metaphysical posture toward Being which has produced the spirit of technicity with all of its baneful consequences. Thus Western metaphysics must be overcome. Since language as λόγος is so intimately tied to Being, a change in our relation to Being must, of necessity, involve a change in our relation to language.

The importance of what Heidegger is saying concerning language can scarcely be overestimated. What he is advocating is no less than a radical transformation of man's relationship to language. Because of his relationship to his world he has exploited it and left it devastated. He has produced an environment which is not fit for *human* dwelling. Just as this relationship must be changed if he is to have a world in which to dwell as man, so also must his relationship to language be changed, since language gives man a human world. If one regards the present crisis in which man finds himself as grave, involving as it does the question of his very survival as man, then what Heidegger says concerning language is indeed of crucial importance.

---

[128] On the poet's role in the overcoming of technicity see my article, "Heidegger on Language: The Role of the Poet and the Thinker," *Knowledge, Culture and Value* (Delhi: Motilal Banarsidass, 1976), vol. II, 455-460.

CONCLUSION

In the voluminous literature that has been written on Heidegger's thought there are two diametrically opposed tendencies. By his critics, on the one hand, there is a tendency to reject his writing out of hand, as unintelligible obscurity which attempts to pass for profundity. If his thought is given careful attention at all, it is with a view to ferreting out inadequacies, shortcomings, or demonstrating the demoralizing effect of a godless mysticism of Being. Accordingly, his thought has been characterized alternately as nihilism, irrationalism, a pietism of Being, empty word-play, nonsense statements, etc.. The other tendency is to regard Heidegger as a kind of philosophical messiah, to accept his writings with the reverence of oracular responses, or a kind of revelation[1] which may not be subjected to the same rules of criticism and examination that may, quite rightly, be demanded of other philosophers. In our evaluation we shall attempt to steer a middle course. A great philosopher, and Heidegger is this if only from the standpoint of the influence he has exercised, ought not to be read as though he were being tried by the Inquisition.[2] He should have at least a fair hearing, and preferably a sympathetic one. But however great a philosopher is, he is not exempt from critical examination. We are not obliged to accept him simply on his own word or on faith. Hence our evaluation will attempt to follow this path — to interpret Heidegger sympathetically, but to face squarely several serious charges that are levelled against him by his critics. To be sure, we shall not attempt to answer all of the objections that have been raised against him, since simply to catalogue them completely would require something like a "syllabus errorum philosophicorum". We shall confine our attention to those points only which seem to be central to the logic problematic. Accordingly, we shall attempt

[1] See for example Jean Guitton, "Visite à Heidegger" *La Table Ronde*, 1958, n. 123, 147; Glicksman, "A Note on the Philosophy of Heidegger ...", pp. 93-104.
[2] Pöggeler, "Sein als Ereignis ...", p. 597.

to take a hard look at Heidegger's position vis-à-vis logic, and to
determine whether or not there is anything of value in it. Does he,
in the last analysis, completely misunderstand what logic is? Does his
criticism of logic lead to irrationalism, the enthronement of feeling and
blind instinct in place of reason? If he rejects the laws of logic as
the ultimate standard of thought is there really any test for this kind
of thinking or is it, in the final reckoning, simply arbitrary?

What does Heidegger understand by logic, and in what sense, if any,
is it compatible with his "way"? In a word, logic for Heidegger,
if it is to be something more than simply relating mental representations
to each other, must be a reflection on λόγος (*Besinnung auf den* λόγος),[3]
in which λόγος is conceived as being united to Being as truth, i.e.
Being in its collectedness by which it comes to presence, and also
λόγος in the sense of language, in which Being is regathered and held
in openness. Could we say that logic understood either as classical
Aristotelian logic or modern logics, is compatible with Heidegger's way
of conceiving of the task of philosophy? In view of the many statements
of Heidegger in which he concedes that logic is a legitimate enterprise,
valuable in its own way,[4] etc., one is tempted in a spirit of philosophic
irenicism to answer in the affirmative. Here we shall eschew the path
of a too facile concordism and answer the question in the negative,
with the following reservation. If by logic one understands a reflection
on λόγος, then of course it is perfectly compatible with his *Denkweg*.
If, however, one takes logic as it has traditionally been understood
and practiced, then one is forced to say that it is incompatible with
Heidegger's way of thought. Why should this be so? Let us recall
briefly several of the salient points of the argument. First, Heidegger's
basic concern from the beginning of his way has been with the meaning
of Being, or Being as truth. Second, the very core of his thought lies
in his understanding of truth as ἀλήθεια, as simultaneous revelation
and self-concealment. Third, the history of Western metaphysics has
been characterized by its singular forgetfulness of the difference between
Being and beings, or Being in its revelatory power as truth. Fourth,
for Heidegger logic is not an accidental accessory in the process of
the forgetfulness of Being but is the very condition for the development
and deepening of the oblivion of Being in its difference. Logic was
in fact born at that precise moment in history when truth as ἀλήθεια

---

[3] DF, p. 122.

[4] See for example DF, pp. 121-122; US, pp. 160-161; WM, p. 47; EM, p. 92;
WD, p. 126.

had been concealed.[5] Indeed, its very birth was caused by this concealing,[6] since it was only on condition of a transformation of the essence of truth, ἀλήθεια, to ἰδέα that its location in the proposition could take place, which in its turn was the necessary pre-condition for the evolution of logic.[7] Hence logic is not simply a mode of the forgetfulness of Being as truth. It is its first effect and the first prerequisite condition for the development of Western metaphysics, which itself, in its very constitution, is logical,[8] i.e. onto-*logical*,[9] and consequently is condemned by its very nature to move in the realm of *Seinsvergessenheit*. From this it should be quite clear that as far as Heidegger himself is concerned in his own quest after Being logic by its very nature could not have any useful role to play. Still, Heidegger does concede in many statements that logic has its own particular value, its use etc., as we noted. But just what would that use be in an authentic philosophy? It would, frankly, be hard to say just in what way it would be at all helpful, given what Heidegger has said about it. The words seem really to be nothing more than an empty lip service.

A further question remains — when Heidegger asserts that logic is a reflection on λόγος, has he not completely misunderstood the nature of logic, as some have objected.[10] What modern, or for that matter classical, logician has recognized his work as a "reflection on λόγος"? None, to be sure. This, however, is not to say that Heidegger has completely misunderstood the nature of logic. As a matter of fact he understands perfectly well what logic is. As we have noted previously, Heidegger from the very beginning of his career as a philosopher, indeed in the first publication of 1912, demonstrated that he was very well acquainted with the new work that was being done in logic by Frege,

---

[5] EM, p. 92.

[6] EM, pp. 92-93, 143.

[7] EM, pp. 92-93, 130-131.

[8] "... die abendländische 'Metaphysik' ist 'Logik' ..." (N, I, p. 530.) Cf. also HW, p. 243; ID, pp. 50-58, 66, 68-73.

[9] Cf. for example the essay *Die onto-theo-logische Verfassung der Metaphysik*, contained in ID, pp. 37-73. The whole essay is devoted to establishing the point that metaphysics is essentially logical.

[10] Thus Heinemann claims that Heidegger has completely misunderstood the logic problem: "Aber kämpft er wirklich gegen die Logik oder nicht vielmehr gegen einen künstlich aufgetakelten Popanz von Logik? Welcher Logiker vermag in dieser Beschreibung sein Denken wiederzufinden? Das logische Denken ein Vorstellen von Seiendem in seinem Sein? ... Hier aber wird sie missdeutet, als habe sie es mit dem Logos und dem Wesen des Logos zu tun." *Existenzphilosophie* ..., p. 97. Cf. also Rolf-Dieter Herman, "Heidegger and Logic", *Sophia*, XXIX (1961), p. 355; Bröcker, "Heidegger und die Logik ...", p. 51.

Husserl, Russell and Whitehead. When he uses the word "logic" he does not employ it in any specialized sense. It has the meaning which has been traditionally associated with it since Aristotle. It is this logic, so Heidegger contends, born of the forgetfulness of Being, which has dominated metaphysics leading it to its logical end-point in Hegel where logic and ontology are identified[11] — it is this logic that must be shaken to its foundation.[12] Thus the overcoming of metaphysics and the overcoming of logic are but the two sides of the same coin — the overcoming of the forgetfulness of Being as truth. When Heidegger asserts that logic is a reflection on λόγος this is not the result of a misconception of the nature of logic. Rather, it states in what sense logic would have a place in his thought. And what place would that be? As traditionally understood, none. Traditional logic, according to Heidegger, enthroned itself as the supreme measure of thought and has dominated metaphysical thinking since Plato. As we indicated in the *Introduction*, and this should be clear by now, what is involved in the changed role of logic in Heidegger's philosophy is nothing less than one whole way of conceiving of the nature of philosophy. Thus Heidegger has not misunderstood logic. He knows perfectly well what logic is, and it is just this, this domineering reason, logic, that must be overcome, at least as Heidegger conceives of the way of philosophy.

Does Heidegger's attempt to "overcome" traditional logic deliver his thought up to irrationalism, the domination of blind instinct, and ultimately to incommunicability?[13] Is it finally reducible to a kind of Pascalian "logique du cœur", as is sometimes argued?[14] To answer these questions two points must be borne in mind. First, Heidegger's statements against logic must be valuated as *polemical* statements. His opponent in the struggle, looked at from Heidegger's point of view, is a kind of *logicism*, an overbearing logic that makes itself the sole judge of what is rational and attempts to dismiss from consideration every facet of reality which cannot be submitted to a strictly conceptual analysis.[15] Let us take for example the most celebrated of his statements on logic, the inaugural address, to which we have referred a number of times. If one recalls the philosophical climate which was in the ascendency at that time in 1929, one can perhaps be a bit more sympathetic.

[11] EM, p. 93.
[12] EM, p. 144.
[13] EM, pp. 93-94.
[14] Gründer, "M. Heideggers Wissenschaftskritik ...", p. 314.
[15] EM, p. 92.

Wittgenstein had published the *Tractatus* in 1921, eight years earlier, and it had had an enormous impact. In the *Tractatus* Wittgenstein had asserted that all metaphysical statements are nonsense[16] with a kind of youthful arrogance which he later came to regret himself.[17] Wittgenstein, though himself never an actual member of the Vienna Circle, was very close to the members of the Circle, especially during the years of his retirement from Cambridge, that is up to 1929. His position with respect to metaphysics being nonsense gained wide currency especially through the writing of A. J. Ayer, particularly in *Language, Truth and Logic*. All of this is saying that there was a very strong anti-metaphysical bias among many logicians at this time, and particularly because of the wide influence that the work of the members of the Vienna Circle was beginning to have in the growth of logical positivism. It is against such a background that one must look at Heidegger's polemical statements on logic. Quite understandably, it would seem, one who is involved in doing foundational ontology does not appreciate being informed that what he is saying is nonsense. Therefore when Heidegger inveighs against logic, as for example in the inaugural address, it must be remembered that the statements are polemical and they must be evaluated as such.

In his later writings, particularly after the Hölderlin lectures of 1936, Heidegger turns his attention more and more to the question of language. Language now seems to provide the best avenue of approach to Being, and the poets seem to furnish a privileged access to language. Hence in his later writings he is more and more at pains to vindicate the rights of a different non-logical, though certainly not illogical, mode of thought — the poetic. Of this approach to Being that is, the poetic, two things can surely be said: 1) it has given mankind some profound glimpses of truth; 2) it has not followed a strictly "logical" method in achieving this. The second point which must be kept in mind, is that Heidegger is attempting a new beginning in philosophy. As we have seen, he views the Platonic-Aristotelian tradition as having reached a point of exhaustion which is manifested in several related ways: in Hegel, in Nietzsche, in the despoliation of man's world by the depredations of technicity, in the instrumentalization of man in a massive impersonal society, and so on. Because he is attempting a new beginning, it is, in his view, especially important to understand the first beginning in

[16] See for example *Tractatus*, 2.172, 2.174, 4.003, 4.12, 4.121.

[17] See the Preface to the *Philosophical Investigations*, trans. G. E. M. Anscombe (Oxford: Blackwell, 1953), p. x. See also nos. 23, 97, 114.

which Being was experienced and expressed by an Anaximander, or a Heraclitus or a Parmenides, not indeed to find out what the past was, but rather to see the past as living in the present and influencing it, and creatively to "repeat" it so as to shape the future according to its authentic possibilities. And hence he reflects upon λόγος as it was originally experienced in the great period of the beginning of Western thought, prior to the birth of logic. He therefore argues, and rightly it would seem, that in the period which preceded Plato and Aristotle thinkers such as Parmenides and Heraclitus thought great thoughts and they did this without the benefit of Aristotelian logic. Although not strictly "logical", one would hesitate to call their thinking irrational, or a giving way to blind instinct.[18] Thus he argues that going back to the original sense of λόγος, does not necessarily entail giving oneself up to irrationalism. What he is suggesting is that there is more than one path to Being. To charge that a way of approaching Being, such as Heidegger's, leads to irrationalism is a risky enterprise at best — it always presupposes that the one who is making it is, of course, on the side of the angels, that he has the measure of what thinking is, and that thought which does not conform to his measure must be rejected.[19] Certainly the great pre-Socratics, the poets, and Eastern thought have not proceeded along strictly "logical" lines. One would, however, be rather reluctant to condemn all of this as "irrational". Thus there seems to be no compelling reason for believing that Heidegger's desire to return to a reflection on λόγος as originally experienced in the beginning of Western thought must inevitably lead to irrationalism.

In insisting on the rights of a way of thought that is close to the poetic[20] does Heidegger's endeavor become a kind of romantic flight from the stern demands imposed by logic, a self-indulgent refusal to achieve clarity and precision? Does he finally end in an incommunicable, mystical pseudo-poetry? These charges also seem to be unjustified. His thought has both "rigor" and "strictness", but, of course, in such an assertion everything depends on what one understands by "strict", and "rigorous". For the most part these terms have been pre-empted by modern logic and science. There doesn't seem to be any compelling reason, however, for such a restrictive usage. It is, it would seem, the result of the emergence of science into a position in which it

[18] HB, p. 39.
[19] WP, pp. 9-11. Cf. also, H. Tint, "Heidegger and the Irrational," *Proceedings of the Aristotelian Society*, LVII (1956-57), 266.
[20] WM, pp. 50-51.

is regarded as the pinnacle of human knowing. It produces results which are tangible — men are, after all, going to the moon, and they can do so only because of *exact* calculation. But while the "exact" thinking of science and logic may be one way of thinking, to say that all thought which does not conform to this standard is guilty of lack of clarity, imprecision and want of strictness, would seem to be a totally unwarranted abridgment of these terms. Heidegger's thought is "strict", he would argue, not in the sense of technical exactitude, but in the "strictness" with which it gives itself to that which is most thought-worthy — Being.[21] Thus logico-scientific thought is no "stricter" than the thought which holds itself out into Being,[22] but simply more "exact", in that as calculative, it reckons up its calculations with perfect exactness.[23] Further, Heidegger's insistence that the logico-scientific way of thinking is not the only way, and indeed not the most meaningful way of thought, has the very great merit of vindicating the lawful rights of other approaches to Being — the poetic and philosophical. In the formalization and symbolization of thought and language, in the interest of exactness of calculation, words and language must be deprived of their flexibility, the richness of their wide range of meanings, emotional resonances and overtones, and rigidly fixed in a symbol. This procedure is, no doubt, necessary for precision in calculation. It makes it possible to computerize the whole operation so that an electronic brain can carry it out with far greater speed and accuracy than the human mind. But where exactness of calculation becomes the predominant concern, the exactness of the thought-machine tends to become the paradigm toward which thinking ought to tend. The activity which had traditionally been uniquely his as man, thinking, has now been usurped by machines. Thinking has become an affair of machines, rather than men. In this process Heidegger sees a threat to man himself. He is in danger of becoming the slave of the machines he himself has created.[24] He is threatened by his scientifico-technological culture with dehumanization.

Hence the importance of the language, logic, and thought questions for Heidegger. Formalization and symbolization of language and thought are certainly legitimate endeavors. The development of computers and electronic brains makes it possible to eliminate much of the drudgery of calculation and one would be foolish to reject this. But to think

[21] WM, p. 47.
[22] HB, pp. 6-7.
[23] WM, pp. 25, 47.
[24] HH, pp. 27-28.

that this approach to language or thought exhausts its full essence, that it is the only way, or indeed the most important one, is another matter altogether. It is with this latter approach that Heidegger has entered the lists.

Philosophy itself has been drawn into the wake of a now all triumphant science whose exact thinking has become the standard for all thinking.[25] Haunted by a fear of losing prestige and being reduced to an inferior status because of its "unscientificness", philosophy attempts to ape the exactness of the sciences, an effort in which it betrays its own essence. Being, as the element in which thought alone can live, has been sacrificed for exactness which can only be achieved by formalization, and while philosophy perhaps achieves a temporary gain in status, it does so by attempting to become what it is not — science.[26] And in this drive to exactness logic is the initial impulse. Concerning this absorption of philosophy (and logic) into science and the trans-formation of the method of philosophy into that of the mathematico-physical sciences, it is a fact, perhaps, of some significance, that the new logic is now taught under the aegis of the departments of mathematics or science at many universities.

Is the thinking which Heidegger proposes as appropriate to philosophy arbitrary because it has rejected logic?[27] Does it have a criterion of truth, a principle of verification by which its truth can be tested? If we understand principle of verification in the narrowly dogmatic sense in which it was originally used by the logicians of the Vienna Circle, in which the truth of a proposition (non-tautological) was regarded as unverifiable unless it could be verified by empirical evidence,[28] we may state categorically that it has no such verifiability. Somewhat later, Carnap in his work *The Logical Syntax of Language* broadened the notion of verifiability in the formulation of the "tolerance principle", so that one was free to choose whatever method of verification seemed appro-priate to the matter.[29] But to talk about verification from *within* the framework of Heidegger's thought one would have to be extremely careful, because verification rests upon a definite conception of truth, that is, truth as agreement, the correspondence of a proposition to a

[25] DF, p. 8.

[26] HB, pp. 6-7.

[27] HB, p. 46.

[28] For perhaps the best known exposition of the verification principle, cf. A. J. Ayer, *Language, Truth and Logic* ..., pp. 31 ff.

[29] Carnap, *Logical Syntax of Language* ..., pp. 51 ff.

state of affairs outside of the mind. In Heidegger, as we have seen, there are three types of truth, the truth of the proposition (*Satzwahrheit*),[30] the truth of beings (*ontische Wahrheit*)[31] and the truth of Being (*ontologische Wahrheit*).[32] The basis of all truth is openness.[33] Thus to verify the truth of the proposition "the picture on the wall is crooked", if one's back is turned, one has simply to turn around and look.[34] But the truth of the proposition rests upon a more primordial base, that is, the openness (*Entdecktheit*)[35] of the being in question. If beings were not somehow open and uncovered to Dasein their truth could not first be known, and then expressed in the proposition.[36] But more original still is the truth of Being itself which discloses itself (*Enthülltheit des Seins*)[37] in lighting up beings and thus making it possible for them to be manifest. The truth of Being is especially oriented toward Dasein, since Dasein is by its very nature open to Being (*Erschlossenheit*),[38] and hence grasps Being's revelation in thought (*Denken*) and holds it open in language (λόγος, *Sprache*). The disclosure of Being, therefore, is found in the thought of the great thinkers and poets. Thus to talk about a principle of verification *within* the Heideggerian circle of thought would not be terribly significant since the concept of a verification principle rests upon the notion of truth as correspondence, which, for Heidegger is an inadequate notion of truth. *Within* a Heideggerian frame of reference the thinker and the poet "verify" the truth through Being's revelation, the basis of which is openness. Looking at Heidegger from the *outside*, one may choose the verification principle which seems appropriate to him — does his descriptive analysis of Being and Dasein seem to be rich in the wealth of its insight and detail, or no.

The final question to which we wish to address ourselves concerns the possibility of a fruitful encounter between those interested in Heidegger's thought and the logicians. Certainly, going back to his address at Freiburg in 1929 and to statements of Wittgenstein in the *Tractatus*, as well as Ayer and Carnap *et al*, it has not gotten off

[30] WG, p. 12.
[31] WG, p. 12.
[32] WG, p. 13.
[33] WG, p. 13.
[34] SZ, p. 217.
[35] WG, p. 13.
[36] SZ, p. 218.
[37] WG, p. 13.
[38] WG, p. 13.

to a very promising start. Certainly as one attends philosophy meetings and congresses there is a sharp division, not to say a seemingly insuperable wall, between these two groups. Rather than a fruitful dialogue between them, in point of fact what usually happens is that communication quickly degenerates into a series of monologues, or perhaps more accurately, harangues, delivered by one side against the other.[39] Certainly, the philosopher, who since time immemorial has been concerned with the pursuit of truth, ought not to reject any path by which it might be achieved. Heidegger likes to think of his philosophy as a "way", and as he has pointed out explicitly, certainly not the *only* way.[40] He has never rejected logic, be it Aristotelian or modern, as being an invalid mode of thought, any more than he has rejected science as being an illegitimate enterprise.[41] He feels, and quite rightly it would seem, since many scientists seem to share his feeling, that in our scientifico-technological age the essence of man is endangered.[42] Thus his concern has been to vindicate as strongly as possible the legitimate rights of another way of thought. At a time in the history of philosophy when modern logistics, an outgrowth of the spirit of technicity as Heidegger sees it, is tending to establish itself as the *only* legitimate way of philosophizing, he has felt compelled to show its limitation and assert the lawful rights of another way. This, however, is not at all to say that all possibility of dialogue between those who find in Heidegger's thought a fruitful approach to Being and the logicians is precluded. Since truth is won with such great difficulty, no path that leads to its discovery should be disdained.

[39] Yehoshua Bar-Hillel, "A Prerequisite for a Rational Philosophical Discussion", *Logic and Language* (Dordrecht: Reidel, 1962), pp. 1-5.

[40] "Ich sage: auf *einen* Weg. Damit geben wir zu, dass dieser Weg gewiss nicht der einzige Weg ist." WP, pp. 7-8. Heidegger's emphasis.

[41] DF, p. 8.

[42] WM, p. 24.

BIBLIOGRAPHY

I. HEIDEGGER BIBLIOGRAPHIES

Gerber, Rudolph. "Focal Points in Recent Heidegger Scholarship," *New Scholasticism*, XLII (1968), 560-577.

Lübbe, Hermann. "Bibliographie der Heidegger-Literatur 1917-1955," *Zeitschrift für philosophische Forschung*, XI (1957), 401-452.

Paumen, Jean. "Eléments de bibliographie Heideggérienne," *Revue Internationale de Philosophie*, XIV (1960), 263-268.

Pereboom, Dirk. "Heidegger Bibliographie 1917-1966," *Freiburger Zeitschrift für Philosophie und Theologie*, XVI (1969), 100-161.

Sass, Hans-Martin. *Heidegger-Bibliographie.* Meisenheim am Glan: Hain, 1968.

—. *Materialien zur Heidegger-Bibliographie 1917-1972.* Meisenheim am Glan: Verlag Anton Hain, 1975.

Schneeberger, Guido. *Ergänzungen zu einer Heidegger-Bibliographie.* Bern: Suhr, 1960.

II. WORKS BY HEIDEGGER

The following is a selective listing of Heidegger's works. For a complete listing of Heidegger's works, as well as his lectures and seminars, in the order both of their composition, and appearance, see Richardson, *Heidegger: Through Phenomenology to Thought*, pp. 663-680.

Aus der Erfahrung des Denkens. Pfullingen: Neske, 1954.

Der Feldweg. 3rd ed. Frankfurt am Main: Klostermann, 1962.

Der Satz vom Grund. 2nd ed. Bern: Francke, 1954.

Die Frage nach dem Ding. Tübingen: Niemeyer, 1962.

Einführung in die Metaphysik. 2nd ed. Tübingen: Niemeyer, 1958.

Erläuterungen zu Hölderlins Dichtung. 2nd ed. Frankfurt am Main: Klostermann, 1951.

"Fragen nach dem Aufenthalt des Menschen," *Neue Zürcher Zeitung*, Nr. 606, 5 Okt. 1969.

Gelassenheit. Pfullingen: Neske, 1959.

Hebel — der Hausfreund. 2nd ed. Pfullingen: Neske, 1958.

Holzwege. 3rd ed. Frankfurt am Main: Klostermann, 1957.

Identität und Differenz. Pfullingen: Neske, 1957.

Kant und das Problem der Metaphysik. 2nd ed. Frankfurt am Main: Klostermann, 1951.

Kants These über das Sein. Frankfurt am Main: Klostermann, 1962.

Die Kategorien- und Bedeutungslehre des Duns Scotus. Tübingen: 1916.

Die Lehre vom Urteil im Psychologismus. Ein kritisch-positiver Beitrag zur Logik. Leipzig: 1914.

Nietzsche. 2 vols. Pfullingen: Neske, 1961.

Phänomenologie und Theologie. Frankfurt a. M.: Klostermann, 1970.

Platons Lehre von der Wahrheit. 2nd ed. Bern: Francke, 1954.

Schellings Abhandlung. Über das Wesen der menschlichen Freiheit (1809). Ed. Hildegard Feick. Tübingen: Niemeyer, 1971.

Sein und Zeit. 8th ed. Tübingen: Niemeyer, 1957.

Über den Humanismus. Frankfurt am Main: Klostermann, 1947.

Unterwegs zur Sprache. Pfullingen: Neske, 1959.

Vom Wesen des Grundes. 4th ed. Frankfurt am Main: Klostermann, 1955.

Vom Wesen der Wahrheit. 3rd ed. Frankfurt am Main: Klostermann, 1954.

Vorträge und Aufsätze. Pfullingen: Neske, 1954.

Was heisst Denken? Tübingen: Niemeyer, 1961.

Was ist Metaphysik? 7th ed. Frankfurt am Main: Klostermann, 1949.

Was ist das — die Philosophie? Pfullingen: Neske, 1956.

Zur Sprache des Denkens. Tübingen: Niemeyer, 1969.

Zur Seinsfrage. Frankfurt am Main: Klostermann, 1956.

"Neuere Forschungen über Logik," *Literarische Rundschau für das katholische Deutschland*, XXXVIII (1912), cols. 465-472, 517-524, 567-570.

"Zeichen," *Neue Zürcher Zeitung*, Nr. 579, 21 Sept. 1969, p. 51.

III. ENGLISH TRANSLATIONS OF HEIDEGGER

The following is a selected listing of English translations of Heidegger's works. For a complete listing of the available translations see, Keith Hoeller, "Heidegger

Bibliography of English Translations," *Journal of the British Society for Phenomenology*, VI (1975), 206-208.

Being and Time. Translated by John Macquarrie and Edward Robinson. New York: Harper & Row, 1962.

Discourse on Thinking. Translated by John Anderson and E. H. Freund. New York: Harper & Row, 1966.

Essays in Metaphysics: Identity and Difference. Translated by Kurt Leidecker. New York: Philosophical Library, 1960.

The Essence of Reasons. Translated by Terrence Malick. Evanston: Northwestern University Press, 1969.

"Hölderlin and the Essence of Poetry," in *Existence and Being.* Translated by Douglas Scott. Chicago: Regnery, 1949.

Introduction to Metaphysics. Translated by Ralph Manheim. New Haven: Yale Univ. Press, 1958.

Kant and the Problem of Metaphysics. Translated by James Churchill. Bloomington: Indiana Univ. Press, 1962.

"Letter on Humanism," in *Philosophy in the Twentieth Century*, Vol. III. Translated by Edgar Lohner. New York: Random House, 1962.

"On the Essence of Truth," in *Existence and Being.* Translated by R. Hull and A. Crick. Chicago: Regnery, 1949.

"Plato's Doctrine of Truth," in *Philosophy in the Twentieth Century*, Vol. III. Translated by J. Barlow. New York: Random House, 1962.

"Remembrance of the Poet," in *Existence and Being.* Translated by Douglas Scott. Chicago: Regnery, 1949.

"The Age of the World View," *Measure*, II (1951), 269-284. Translated by Marjorie Grene.

"The Origin of a Work of Art," in *Philosophies of Art and Beauty.* Translated by A. Hofstadter. New York: Random House, 1965.

The Question of Being. Translated by W. Kluback and J. T. Wilde. New York: Twayne, 1959.

"The Way Back into the Ground of Metaphysics," in *Existentialism from Dostoevski to Sartre.* Translated by Walter Kaufmann. New York: Meridian, 1957.

What Is a Thing. Translated by W. B. Barton and Vera Deutsch. Chicago: Regnery, 1967.

What is Called Thinking. Translated by F. Wieck and J. G. Gray. New York: Harper & Row, 1962.

"What is Metaphysics?" in *Existence and Being.* Translated by R. Hull and Alan Crick. Chicago: Regnery, 1949.

What is Philosophy? Translated by W. Kluback and J.T. Wilde. New York: Twayne, 1958.

The End of Philosophy. Translated by Joan Stambaugh. New York: Harper & Row, 1973.

Poetry, Language and Thought. Translated by Albert Hofstadter. New York: Harper & Row, 1971.

On the Way to Language. Translated by Peter Hertz. New York: Harper & Row, 1971.

On Time and Being. Translated by Joan Stambaugh. New York: Harper & Row, 1972.

"The Idea of Phenomenology," *New Scholasticism*, XLIV (1970), 325-344. Translated by John Deely and Joseph Novak.

Hegel's Concept of Experience. New York: Harper & Row, 1970.

Early Greek Thinking. Translated by David Farrell Krell and Frank Capuzzi. New York: Harper & Row, 1975.

"Kant's Thesis About Being," *Southwestern Journal of Philosophy* IV (1973), 7-33. Translated by Ted E. Klein and William E. Pohl.

"Nietzsche as Metaphysician", in *Nietzsche: A Collection of Critical Essays*, ed. Robert C. Solomon, translated by Joan Stambaugh. Garden City: Doubleday, 1973, pp. 105-113.

"The Pathway", *Listening*, II (1967), 88-91. Translated by Thomas F. O'Meara.

The Piety of Thinking. Translated by James G. Hart and John Maraldo. Bloomington: Indiana University Press, 1975.

"The Principle of Ground", *Man and World*, VII (1974), 207-222. Translated by Keith Hoeller.

The Question Concerning Technology: Heidegger's Critique of the Modern Age. Translated by William Lovitt. New York: Harper & Row, 1977.
Arthur.

IV. SECONDARY SOURCES CITED IN THE TEXT

Adkins, Arthur, "Heidegger and Language," *Philosophy*, XXXVII (1962), 229-237.

Apel, Karl-Otto. "Sprache und Wahrheit in der gegenwärtigen Situation der Philosophie," *Philosophische Rundschau*, VII (1957), 161-184.

—. "Die Entfaltung der 'sprachanalytischen' Philosophie und das Problem der 'Geisteswissenschaften,'" *Philosophisches Jahrbuch*, LXXII (1965), 239-289.

—. "Wittgenstein und das Problem des hermeneutischen Verstehens," *Zeitschrift für Theologie und Kirche*, LXIII (1966), 49-87.

—. "Wittgenstein und Heidegger: Die Frage nach dem Sinn von Sein und der Sinnlosigkeitsverdacht gegen alle Metaphysik," *Philosophisches Jahrbuch*, LXXV (1967), 56-94.

Ayer, A. J. *Language, Truth and Logic*. New York: Dover, 1946.

Bar-Hillel, Yehoshua. "A Prerequisite for Rational Discussion," *Logic and Language*. Studies Dedicated to Rudolf Carnap on the Occasion of His Seventieth Birthday. Edited by B. Z. Kazemier and D. Vuysje. Dordrecht: Reidel, 1962.

Birault, Henri. "Existence et vérité d'après Heidegger," *Revue de Métaphysique et Morale*, LVI (1950), 35-87.

—. "Heidegger et la pensée de la finitude," *Revue Internationale de Philosophie*, XIV (1960), 135-162.

Bochénski, I. M. *Formale Logik*. Freiburg/München: Orbis Academicus, 1956.

Boeder, H. "Der frühgriechische Wortgebrauch von Logos und Aletheia," *Archiv für Begriffsgeschichte*, IV (1959), 82-112.

Boehm, Rudolf. "Pensée et technique," *Revue Internationale de Philosophie*, XIV (1960), 194-220.

Borgmann, Albert. "Heidegger and Symbolic Logic," *Heidegger and the Quest for Truth*. Edited by Manfred Frings. Chicago: Quadrangle, 1968.

Bröcker, Walter. "Heidegger und die Logik," *Philosophische Rundschau*, I (1953-54), 48-56.

Buddeberg, Else. *Heidegger und die Dichtung: Hölderlin und Rilke*. Stuttgart: Metzlesche, 1953.

Carnap, Rudolf. "Überwindung der Metaphysik durch logische Analyse der Sprache," *Erkenntnis*, II (1932), 219-24.

—. *Meaning and Necessity: A Study in Semantics and Modal Logic*. Vol. III. Chicago: Univ. of Chicago Press, 1947.

—. "Intellectual Autobiography," *The Philosophy of Rudolf Carnap*. Edited by Paul Schlipp. La Salle: Open Court, 1963.

Carnap, Rudolf, *et al. Wissenschaftliche Weltauffassung: Der Wiener Kreis*. Wien: Artur Wolf, 1929.

Chapelle, Albert. *L'Ontologie phénoménologique de Heidegger*. Paris: Editions Universitaires, 1962.

Corvez, Maurice. *La Philosophie de Heidegger*. Paris: Presses Universitaires de France, 1961.

Demske, James. *Sein, Mensch und Tod. Das Todesproblem bei Martin Heidegger*. München: Alber, 1963.

Dondeyne, Albert. "La différence ontologique chez M. Heidegger," *Revue Philosophique de Louvain*, LVI (1958), 35-62, 251-293.

Fay, Thomas A., "Early Heidegger and Wittgenstein on 'World'", *Philosophical Studies*, XXI (1973), 161-172.

—. "Heidegger on Language: The Role of the Poet and the Thinker," *Knowledge, Culture and Value*. Delhi: Motilal Banarsidass, 1976, vol. II, 455-460.

—. "Heidegger on Logic: A Genetic Study of his Thought", *Journal of the History of Philosophy*, XII (1974), 77-95.

—. "Heidegger: Thinking as *NOEIN*", *Modern Schoolman*, LI (1973), 17-29.

—. "The History of Western Metaphysics as the 'Forgetfulness of Being': A Thomistic Rejoinder," *Atti: Congresso Internazionale Tommaso D'Aquino nel suo VII Centenario*, 1974. Rome.

—. "Heidegger: The Man-Nature Problematic," *Proceedings of the International Society for Metaphysics*, 1976. (forthcoming).

—. "Heidegger: The Role of Logic in His Thought," *Journal of the British Society for Phenomenology*, VIII (1977), n. 2.

—. "Heidegger: The Origin and Development of Symbolic Logic," *Kant-Studien*, (forthcoming).

Feick, Hildegard. *Index zu Heideggers Sein und Zeit*. 2nd rev. ed. Tübingen: Niemeyer, 1968.

Fink, Eugen. "Philosophie als Überwindung der Naivität," *Lexis*, I (1948), 107-127.

Friedländer, Paul. *Plato*. Translated by Hans Meyerhoff. Vol. I. New York: Pantheon, 1958.

Gadamer, Hans-Georg. "Vom Zirkel des Verstehens," *Martin Heidegger zum siebzigsten Geburtstag: Festschrift*. Pfullingen: Neske, 1959.

—. *Wahrheit und Methode: Grundzüge einer philosophischen Hermeneutik*. Tübingen: Mohr, 1960.

Gipper, Helmut. *Bausteine zur Sprachinhaltsforschung*. Düsseldorf: Schwann, 1963.

Glicksman, Marjorie. "A Note on the Philosophy of Heidegger," *Journal of Philosophy*, XXXV (1938), 93-104.

Gochet, P. "La Nature du principe de contradiction," *Memorias del XIII Congreso Internacional de Filosofia*, V (1964), 469-484.

Gray, Glenn. "Poets and Thinkers: Their Kindred Roles in the Philosophy of Martin Heidegger," *Phenomenology and Existentialism*. Edited by Edward Lee and Maurice Mandelbaum. Baltimore: Johns Hopkins Press, 1967.

Gründer, Karlfried. "M. Heideggers Wissenschaftskritik in ihren geschichtlichen Zusammenhängen," *Archiv für Philosophie*, XI (1962), 312-335.

Guilead, Ruben. *Le Problème de la liberté chez Heidegger*. Louvain: Nauwelaerts, 1965.

Guzzoni, Alfredo. "Ontologische Differenz und Nichts," *Martin Heidegger zum siebzigsten Geburtstag: Festschrift*. Pfullingen: Neske, 1959.

Habermas, Jürgen. "Zur Logik der Sozialwissenschaften," *Philosophische Rundschau*, Beiheft V, 1967.

Harries, Karsten. "Heidegger and Hölderlin: The Limits of Language," *Personalist*, XLIV (1963), 5-23.

—. "Wittgenstein and Heidegger: The Relationship of the Philosopher to Language," *Journal of Value Inquiry*, II (1968), 281-291.

Heinemann, Fritz. *Existenzphilosophie — lebendig oder tot?* Stuttgart: Kohlhammer, 1963.

Heitsch, E. "Wahrheit als Erinnerung," *Hermes*, XCI (1963), 36-53.

—. "Die nicht-philosophische Aletheia," *Hermes*, XC (1962), 24-33.

Hermann, Rolf-Dieter. "Heidegger and Logic," *Sophia*, XXIX (1961), 353-357.

Hollenbach, Johannes. *Sein und Gewissen*. Baden-Baden: Grimm, 1954.

Horgby, Ingvar. "The Double Awareness in Heidegger and Wittgenstein," *Inquiry*, II (1959), 235-264.

Huch, Kurt Jürgen. *Philosophiegeschichtliche Voraussetzungen der Heideggerschen Ontologie*. Frankfurt am Main: Europäische Verlagsanstalt, 1967.

Kaufmann, Walter. *From Shakespeare to Existentialism*. New York: Doubleday, 1960.

Kneale, William, and Kneale, Martha. *The Development of Logic*. Oxford: Clarendon, 1962.

Kockelmans, Joseph. "Thanks-giving: The Completion of Thought," *Heidegger and the Quest for Truth*. Edited by Manfred Frings. Chicago: Quadrangle Books, 1967.

Koza, Ingeborg. *Das Problem des Grundes in Heideggers Auseinandersetzung mit Kant*. Ratingen bei Düsseldorf: A. Henn, 1967.

Kraft, Victor. *Der Wiener Kreis: Der Ursprung des Neupositivismus*. Wien: Springer, 1950.

Kruger, Gerhard. "Martin Heidegger und der Humanismus," *Studia Philosophica*, IX (1949), 93-129.

Kuhn, Helmut. "Heideggers 'Holzwege'," *Archiv für Philosophie*, IV (1952), 253-269.

Küng, Guido. *Ontology and the Logistic Analysis of Language*. Dordrecht: Reidel, 1967.

Laffoucrière, Odette. *Le Destin de la pensée et "La Mort de Dieu" selon Heidegger*. La Haye: Nijhoff, 1968.

Levinas, Emmanuel. *En découvrant l'existence avec Husserl et Heidegger*. Paris: Vrin, 1949.

Lingis, A. F. "On the Essence of Technique," *Heidegger and the Quest for Truth.* Edited by Manfred Frings. Chicago: Quadrangle Books, 1967.

Logic and Language. First and Second Series. Edited by Anthony Flew. Garden City: Doubleday, 1965.

Logical Positivism. Edited by A. J. Ayer. Glencoe: Free Press, 1959.

Löwith, Karl. *Heidegger: Denker in dürftiger Zeit.* Göttingen: Vandenhoeck & Ruprecht, 1960.

Marx, Werner. "Heidegger's New Conception of Philosophy: The Second Phase of Existentialism," *Social Research,* XXII (1955), 451-474.

—. *Heidegger und die Tradition.* Stuttgart: Kohlhammer, 1961.

McLean, George. "Chronicle I: Vienna and Gallarate — 1968," *New Scholasticism,* XLIII (1969), 282-293.

Médicis, Stelios Castanos De. *Réponse à Heidegger sur l'humanisme.* Paris: Pedone, 1966.

Müller, Max. *Existenzphilosophie im geistigen Leben der Gegenwart.* Heidelberg: Kerle, 1964.

Neurath, Otto. *Le développement du Cercle de Vienne et l'avenir de l'empirisme logique.* Paris: Hermann, 1935.

Ott, Heinrich. *Denken und Sein: Der Weg Martin Heideggers und der Weg der Theologie.* Zollikon: Evangelischer Verlag, 1959.

Otto, Walter. "Die Zeit und Das Sein," *Anteile: Martin Heidegger zum 60. Geburtstag.* Frankfurt am Main: Klostermann, 1950.

Pöggeler, Otto. *Der Denkweg Martin Heideggers.* Pfullingen: Neske, 1963.

—. "Sein als Ereignis," *Zeitschrift für philosophische Forschung,* XIII (1959), 597-632.

Richardson, William J., S. J. "A Letter from Heidegger, with Commentary and Translation by W. J. Richardson, S. J.," *Heidegger and the Quest for Truth.* Edited by Manfred Frings. Chicago: Quadrangle Books, 1968.

—. "Heidegger and God — and Professor Jonas," *Thought,* XL (1965), 13-40.

—. "Heidegger and the Origin of Language," *International Philosophical Quarterly,* II (1962), 404-416.

—. "Heidegger and the Problem of Thought," *Revue Philosophique de Louvain,* LX (1962), 58-78.

—. "Heidegger and Theology," *Theological Studies,* XXVI (1965), 86-100.

—. "Heidegger's Critique of Science," *New Scholasticism,* XLII (1968), 511-536.

—. *"Heidegger: Through Phenomenology to Thought.* The Hague: Nijhoff, 1963.

—. "Heideggers Weg durch die Phänomenologie zum Seinsdenken," *Philosophisches Jahrbuch,* LXII (1965), 385-396.

—. "Kant and the Later Heidegger," *Phenomenology in America*. Edited by James Edie. Chicago: Quadrangle Books, 1967.

Richey, Clarence. "On the Intentional Ambiguity of Heidegger's Metaphysics," *Journal of Philosophy*, LV (1958), 1144-1148.

Ricœur, Paul. "Husserl and Wittgenstein on Language," *Phenomenology and Existentialism*. Edited by Edward Lee and Maurice Mandelbaum. Baltimore: Johns Hopkins Press, 1967.

—. *History and Truth*. Translated by Charles Kelbley. Evanston: Northwestern Univ. Press, 1965.

—. "The Critique of Subjectivity and the Cogito in the Philosophy of Heidegger," *Heidegger and the Quest for Truth*. Edited by Manfred Frings. Chicago: Quadrangle Books, 1968.

Rioux, Bertrand. *L'Être et la vérité chez Heidegger et S. Thomas d'Aquin*. Paris: Presses Universitaires de France, 1963.

Schulz, Walter. "Über den philosophiegeschichtlichen Ort Martin Heideggers," *Philosophische Rundschau*, I(1953-54), 65-93, 211-232.

Seidel, George. *Martin Heidegger and the Presocratics*. Lincoln: Univ. of Nebraska Press, 1964.

Smith, Joseph. "In-the-World and on-the-Earth," *Heidegger and the Quest for Truth*. Edited by Manfred Frings. Chicago: Quadrangle Books, 1967.

Spiegelberg, Herbert. *The Phenomenological Movement*. 2 vols. The Hague: Nijhoff, 1960.

The Later Heidegger and Theology. Edited by James Robinson and John Cobb. New York: Harper & Row, 1963.

Tugendhat, Ernst. *Der Wahrheitsbegriff bei Husserl und Heidegger*. Berlin: De Gruyter, 1967.

Friedrich Weismann: Wittgenstein und der Wiener Kreis. Edited by B. F. McGuinness. Oxford: Blackwell, 1967.

I. INDEX OF GREEK TERMS

II. INDEX OF GERMAN TERMS

The following listing includes only those page references where the actual German words occur in the text, and not where the translations of the notions contained in the German words occur.

III. INDEX OF PROPER NAMES

IV. GENERAL INDEX

and 'Tolerance principle', 117.

and Verification principle, 117, 118.

as agreement between Perceiving and the thing Perceived (correspondence), 70, 71, 72, 117.

as correctness, 70, 71.

as formally found in judgment act, 71.

as openness, 118.

as revelation and concealment, 6, 12, 14, 16, 20, 34, 36, 47, 49, 50, 53, 54, 58, 59, 70, 111.

as a tool for science, 20-21.

as unhiddeness, 70, 71, 98, 104, 111, 112.

Truth, criterion of, 117.

Truth, the essence of, 70.

Truth, its need of man, 34.

of Being, 62, 69, 71, 90, 102, 104, 105, 111, 117.

propositional, 6, 16, 20, 21, 26, 27, 28, 50-51, 71, 118.

scholastic definition, 26-27, 50-51, 71.

"Turn" in Heidegger's way, 105, 106.

Understanding, as power of binding together representations, 75, 76, 77.

Untruth, as the essence of truth, 58.

Vienna Circle, 3, 37, 114, 117.

"Will to Will', 89.

World, 23, 29, 31.

World, as object, 72.